# THE BRIGHTON BELLE

STEPHEN GRANT AND SIMON JEFFS

Capital Transport

No. 7777

# The Pullman Car Company, Ltd.

PASSENGER'S CHECK. Good for this Trip only when accompanied by a Third-class Railway Ticket.

PASSENGERS ARE EARNESTLY REQUESTED TO SEE THAT TICKETS ARE TORN FROM A BOOK, CORRECTLY FILLED IN, SIGNED AND DATED, AND KINDLY DESTROY THE TICKET AT THE END OF THE JOURNEY.

"BRIGHTON BELLE" One Seat
LONDON TO BRIGHTON
BRIGHTON TO LONDON

1/-        4 193....

......................CONDUCTOR.

SEE CONDITIONS AT BACK.

ACKNOWLEDGEMENTS

Simon would like to thank all the photographers, Pullman enthusiasts and organisations for providing material for this book. Special thanks to John Scrace, Clinton Shaw and Michael Baker for providing so many of the wonderful photos; Antony Ford for visiting me with his precious collection of Belle artefacts to photograph and scan; Denis Dunstone and Neil Marshall of the Transport Trust and all the supporters of the 5Bel Project for their visionary project to bring the Belle back; the Bluebell Railway for allowing Colin Duff, Laurel and I free access to *Doris* at Horsted Keynes; the Railway Performance Society for the performance logs and, finally, my wife Laurel for losing me to long hours staring at a computer screen while assembling this book.

Stephen would also like to thank the many people who contributed factual material, anecdotes and pictures to the book and to salute the small but dedicated band of enthusiasts who are working hard to restore Southern Electric trains to operating condition. Thanks, too, to my wife Anne for her amused tolerance of my distracted attention over a long period of time to Audrey, Doris, Gwen, Hazel, Mona, Vera and the other Brighton Belles.

First published 2011

ISBN 978-185414-346-4

Published by Capital Transport Publishing
www.capitaltransport.com

Printed by 1010 Printing International Ltd

# Contents

# Chapter 1
# Beginnings

Brighton had been a fishing town in decline until, in the 18th century, Dr Richard Russell pronounced that drinking and bathing in sea-water could cure an astonishingly wide variety of illnesses, ranging from constipation and 'fluxions' to incipient insanity.

King George III took the waters at Weymouth, though with no obvious benefit to that unfortunate monarch's state of health. His son, the Prince of Wales and the future George IV, made frequent trips to Brighton to bathe and to pursue his gambling, drinking and amorous affairs out of sight of his censorious father. He adapted and extended a seafront farmhouse to become his neo-classical Marine Pavilion and later commissioned the architect John Nash to further extend and rebuild this pleasure-dome into the exotic Royal Pavilion that still stands today as one of Brighton's principal visitor attractions.

Royal patronage made Brighton a fashionable resort – close enough to London for the journey by coach not to be too daunting but far enough away to maintain exclusivity. Wealthy visitors could dance and play cards in spacious new Assembly Rooms. Areas to the east and the west of the original town were developed in elegant style and a chain pier was built from which, for a time, a steamship operated to France. The new watering-place made an impression on society – Jane Austen alluded to it in a novel that she was writing just before she died in 1817.

Meanwhile, in the less genteel surroundings of the Cornish tin mines, Richard Trevithick was finding out how to apply the steam force of Newcomen and Watt's ponderous, stationary beam engines in a high-pressure mobile power-pack. In 1804 he demonstrated a practical steam locomotive and the idea was taken forward by others, notably George Stephenson. The Stockton and Darlington railway opened for traffic in 1825 with a mix of steam and horse power, followed in 1831 by the world's first inter-city passenger and freight steam railway, from Liverpool to Manchester. Fuelled by the Industrial Revolution's pent-up demand for low-cost transport and by *laissez-faire* capitalism at its most uninhibited, Britain's railway network grew at an explosive rate.

The railway reached Brighton from London Bridge in September 1841. It was a superbly engineered line, with John Rastrick's beautiful viaduct over the River Ouse and three long tunnels at Merstham, Balcombe and Clayton, the last with castellated porticos. The route of the future 'Brighton Belle', from Victoria rather than London Bridge, was not completed until 1862. At Brighton, the architect David Mocatta designed an Italianate station frontage to be complemented from 1882 by a beautifully-proportioned train shed that followed the curved alignment of the platforms.

As early as 1844, the London, Brighton and South Coast Railway (LBSCR) was offering First Class season tickets from Brighton to London Bridge at £50 *per annum*. To cater for this market the company laid on an all-First Class express, the forerunner of the future 'City Limited', which left Brighton at 8.45am and made the journey to London Bridge in 90 minutes. The return working left London Bridge at 4.40pm and reached Brighton at 6.15pm. Already Brighton was within commuting distance of London. The LBSCR also encouraged day trippers to Brighton, the regular service being supplemented during the summer by briskly-timed excursion trains made up of open-sided Third Class carriages. The railway had strengthened and expanded the economic and social association between the capital and this raffishly-elegant resort and this in turn created more demand for high-quality passenger services.

Opposite: The Brighton Terminus of the London & Brighton Railway, c 1845. Designed by David Mocatta the station was built high on the western slope of the valley, through which the road from London entered the town. *NRM/Science & Society Picture Library*

Meanwhile, in America, the railroad network was also growing rapidly. George Mortimer Pullman worked as a travelling salesman for his brother's cabinet-making firm, where he developed an appreciation both of fine craftsmanship and of the rigours of long distance railroad travel. Perceiving a market for something better than the spartan passenger saloons of the North American railroads of the day, Pullman developed and refined the concept of the sleeping car. By the 1860s he had placed fleets of cars, built in his own works, with several North American long-distance railroads which hauled them in their own trains and maintained the running gear. Pullman passengers paid the basic fare to the railroad and a supplement to the Pullman company for the enhanced comfort of these convertible day/sleeping cars and for the services of an attendant.

In 19th century America, as in Britain, long-distance trains used to make brief stops to enable passengers to bolt a hasty meal at the station refreshment room. With their captive markets these, and by association railway catering in general, became a byword for poor quality food and service. Mindful of this, Pullman built his first 'Hotel Car' in 1867, being a convertible day/sleeper with kitchen where a chef would prepare food for the occupants during the journey. At mealtimes, the attendant would put up tables between the seats and set them with linen tablecloths and fine crockery and cutlery.

From this, it was a logical step to providing dining cars, available to all passengers on a day train, and the name 'Pullman' became synonymous with a superior form of rail catering.

Under its General Manager James Allport, Britain's Midland Railway was also developing a reputation for comfort. Allport was familiar with Pullman's operations in America and in 1873 Pullman contracted with the Midland to supply 16 cars for its main-line services. These were a mix of convertible day/sleeping cars for Anglo-Scottish routes and 'Parlour Cars' for shorter-distance journeys. Built in the Pullman Standard factory near Chicago and re-assembled in the Midland's Derby works, these cars closely followed contemporary American practice with a large saloon body mounted on bogies and with open verandas at each end. However the British public, or at least that part of it that could afford a First Class fare and a supplement, was initially slow to warm to the saloon format, with many preferring the semi-privacy of a compartment. From an operating point of view, the Pullman cars were heavy; about twice the weight per passenger of a contemporary British compartment vehicle. These were serious disadvantages given the relatively small locomotives and light track of the time, and the Midland eventually phased out its Pullman operations in favour of providing its own sleeping and restaurant cars. It did, however, purchase some of the Pullman cars and take them into its own stock.

# Chapter 2
# Brighton Line Pullmans

The LBSCR always was rather superior. In Oscar Wilde's 1895 play, 'The Importance of Being Ernest', Jack admits to having been left as a baby in a handbag at London's Victoria station adding, by way of mitigation, 'the Brighton line'. As Hamilton Ellis points out[1], when Lady Bracknell retorts 'the line is immaterial' she is quite wrong – an inferior foundling would have been discovered on the Chatham line's adjacent premises.

In 1875, the Pullman company approached the LBSCR Board with a proposal to operate a Pullman car between Victoria and Brighton. Newly-built 'Mars' was chosen – it had been built as a sleeping car for the Midland but was operated on the LBSCR as a parlour car. This experiment must have been a success because three more cars – 'Alexandra', 'Albert Edward' and 'Globe' were added to the LBSCR-hauled fleet over the next couple of years.

Given the origins of the Pullman brand as a comfortable means of long-distance travel, it is perhaps surprising that the company should come to be associated for almost a century with the Brighton line, one of the shortest main lines in Britain. Yet one can see how it came to succeed so well here. The LBSCR had already developed a market for commuting between an office in the smoky city and a family home in the healthy air of the Sussex coast. For these wealthy gentlemen commuters, the Pullman Parlour Cars had something of the ambience of a London club. Ladies travelling alone found the open layout and the presence of an attendant more secure and reassuring than a compartment in a non-corridor carriage. And for pleasure seekers, perhaps looking to impress their travelling companions, a Pullman car had style.

Pleased with the commercial success of the individual Parlour Cars, Pullman and the LBSCR launched their first all-Pullman express in 1881, operating between London and Brighton twice daily in each direction. The train was made up of four cars, named 'Beatrice', 'Louise', 'Maud' and 'Victoria' in honour of children of the Royal family. 'Beatrice' was the former 'Globe' and the other three cars were re-named trans-

fers from the Midland line. Though not new, the refurbished cars had several innovations. 'Victoria' incorporated a small pantry buffet for the service of tea and sandwiches and the four cars were heated by oil-fired hot water systems – previously the best the winter traveller could hope for was a pre-heated foot-warmer. Perhaps most significantly in view of later developments, the train was lit by electricity. Edison lamps were powered by Fauré accumulator cells pre-charged by a steam-driven dynamo at Victoria and sufficient for six hours of operation.

The inaugural run of this 'Pullman Limited Express' took place on 11th December 1881 – a Sunday. This earned the train the nickname of the 'Sabbath-breaker' among those who considered that making such a journey – to Brighton! … On a Sunday!! – was clear evidence of moral degeneracy. In fact, Sunday patronage proved to be so light that this service was withdrawn after a short time.

In 1887, the British Pullman Palace Car Company – a subsidiary formed five years earlier – ordered three all-new cars from the American parent's Illinois factory specifically for the Brighton line. Shipped in 'knocked down' form, these were assembled by the LBSCR at their Brighton works (the Pullman Company's own workshop at Preston Park was to come later). These cars, 'Prince', 'Princess' and 'Albert Victor', incorporated several further developments. They were fitted with the Westinghouse automatic air brake, a system that the LBSCR was in process of adopting as a standard for all of its passenger fleet. The three were semi-permanently coupled together by means of American MCB standard 'Buckeye' centre-couplers and what was to become known as the Pullman gangway – a sprung vertical end-frame that both provided a safe passage from one car to the next and acted as a buffer to absorb shocks and reduce swaying. Like the 1881 train, these cars were lit by electricity but, following successful experiments by William Stroudley, the LBSCR's Chief Mechanical Engineer of the day, the power source was now a dynamo turned by an axle-driven belt. The dynamo was mounted in the so-called 'Pullman Pup', a guard's and luggage van supplied by the LBSCR but styled and painted to match the Pullman cars.

---

1   Hamilton Ellis, C. 'The London Brighton and South Coast Railway' London: Ian Allan, 1960, p11.

LBSCR Class H1 4-4-2 no. 41 at Brighton with the Southern Belle. The painting is by 'F Moore', the collective name of a studio of artists operating in the first two decades of the 20th century who produced many paintings and painted photographs of steam locomotives prior to the advent of colour photography. *NRM/Science & Society Picture Library*

This set was followed in 1895 by three more cars, 'Her Majesty', 'Duchess of York' and 'Princess of Wales' together with an accompanying Pup, thus providing two complete sets for Brighton line services, though in practice these sets often operated in trains that also included non-Pullman LBSCR stock. The earlier cars, suitably updated, also continued in service and often operated singly on LBSCR services to Brighton, Eastbourne and Hastings or on 'boat trains' to Newhaven that connected with        channel steamers to France.

In 1898 the LBSCR re-launched its Sunday Pullman service to Brighton, originally as the 'Sunday Pullman Limited' but soon renamed the 'Brighton Limited'. This was a genuinely all-Pullman train, First Class only plus supplement. Pullman cars 'Her Majesty', 'Duchess of York' and 'Princess of Wales' were paired with the earlier 'Beatrice' and 'Victoria' and flanked by the two Pups. Hauled by no. 206 'Smeaton', one of the LBSCR's elegant new Class B2 4-4-0 express locomotives designed by Robert Billinton, the inaugural run was completed in just 60 minutes. Times had changed since the 1881 train was condemned as the Sabbath-breaker. This was the Naughty Nineties, the era of Aubrey Beardsley's beautifully decadent

artwork and Oscar Wilde's wittily amoral plays, whilst the rigid social structures of the high-Victorian era were being challenged by first stirrings of the suffragette movement. The new Sunday service was an instant success.

Though it had so far failed to prosper on the other British main lines, Pullman was going from strength to strength on the LBSCR, so much so that more new cars were quickly ordered. 'The Arundel' and 'The Chichester' (1899), 'Devonshire' (1900), 'Duchess of Norfolk', 'Princess Ena' and 'Princess Patricia' (all 1906) were the last Pullmans to be supplied from the Illinois factory and the last with clerestory roofs, but in many ways they were the prototypes of the classic British Pullman car of the 20th century. Mounted on tri-axle bogies and with 64ft long bodies, these impressive cars had large, rectangular windows to each seating bay, electric lighting and kitchens with gas cooking.

Such was the close relationship between the LBSCR and Pullman that the 1906 cars adopted a new livery of umber brown – a shade that matched the LBSCR's latest livery – and cream upper panels. With the later addition of an umber strip at cantrail level, this was to be the standard livery for all British Pullmans until the mid 1960s.

# Chapter 3
# The 'Southern Belle'

Mr Davison Dalziel, financier and *President du Conseil* of the *Compagnie Internationale des Wagons-Lits*, successfully acquired Pullman's UK business in 1907. He bought it through his own company, Drawing Room Cars, and floated it in 1915 as the Pullman Car Co. Ltd. Dalziel brought new energy to a business that had previously been peripheral to Pullman's North American empire, his strategy being to build on the success of the LBSCR operations as a basis for expansion within Britain. As a first step, he awarded a contract to the Birmingham-based Metropolitan Amalgamated Carriage and Wagon Co. Ltd. to construct seven sumptuous new 12-wheel cars to operate the 'Southern Belle', a new daily all-Pullman express service to Brighton.

The new cars were a further development of the 1899-1906 build, less obviously American in appearance as they had a plain domed roof in place of the former clerestory. Each car was 63ft 10ins long, 8ft 8¾ins wide and 13ft 2ins high, weighing between 39 and 42 tons[2]. The two end cars, 'Verona' and 'Alberta' included a guard's compartment with room for luggage. Electricity was supplied from underfloor accumulators on each car, charged by axle-driven dynamos. The cars were heated by a supply of low-pressure steam from the locomotive, in line with emerging standard practice on UK railways. Instead of the lifting windows of earlier cars, these had ventilators above large, square, fixed windows as well as a supply of warmed, filtered fresh air through ventilator ducts.

---

2   Haresnape, B.: 'Pullman – Travelling in Style'. Ian Allan 1987 p80–82

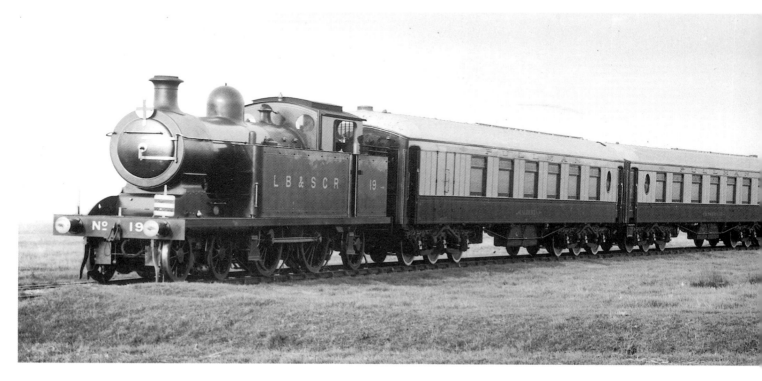

Interior of the 1908 Southern Belle car 'Belgravia', taken from the Southern Belle publicity brochure.

A publicity shot of the new 1908 Pullman cars, the first to be built without American-style clerestory roofs and the forerunners of Pullman car design up to the 1950s. The picture was taken on the Crumbles industrial branch line near Eastbourne, a flat and featureless location often used by the LBSCR for posed photographs. The locomotive, class I2 4-4-2 tank no. 19, was built in the same year but was intended for suburban and local services. The LBSCR did, however, go on to build large-wheeled tank locomotives that were frequently used on expresses such as the 'Southern Belle'. *NRM/Burtt Collection*

Interior of 1908 Pullman car 'Grosvenor'
showing the transverse bar.
*Illustration from the 'Southern Belle'
introductory brochure.*

Internally, the cars were furnished in three different decorative styles. The 'Verona' and 'Alberta' were described as 'French Renaissance', the 'Princess Helen', 'Grosvenor' and 'Bessborough' were finished in the Adam style and the 'Belgravia' and 'Cleopatra' were based on the 18th century decorative work of Michelangelo Pergolesi. 'Grosvenor' included a central kitchen and pantry from which stewards collected meals, sandwiches, beverages, etc., to be served to customers at their seats throughout the train. It also had a small transverse bar for the sale of items such as cigars.

The Southern Belle, which Dalziel claimed to be the 'world's most luxurious train', was launched on 1st November 1908 with a fanfare of publicity. A brochure gushed: *'Upon entering the Southern Belle we leave London behind ... we have come to a place of enchantment, of beauty and exquisite comfort there are many cosy corners where two young people may sit at ease in a snug way and say to each other those vastly important things which belong to the philosophy of youth and love ... the girl pretty and charmingly dressed and with very bright eyes, the man smart and well-groomed ... as the train speeds on its way the sun shines through the window upon them, bathing them in a golden glamour ... but old or young, tired or full of health and vigour, all are at their ease and delighted with this train which provides every conceivable luxury and is exquisite in its artistic decoration'.* The brochure concluded on a more mercenary note: *'all these advantages of a swift and delightful journey may be obtained for 12 shillings, the cost of a return ticket'.*

So successful was the 'Southern Belle' that it was soon making two return trips to Brighton each day, three on Sundays. A further two similar cars, 'Vivienne' and 'Myrtle', the latter described as a buffet car, were added in 1911 to help cope with peak demand. The LBSCR had no restaurant or buffet cars of its own so Pullman cars, individually or in pairs, provided on-board catering on many of the company's other principal services between London and the coast. From 1908, four of the older cars operated the 'Eastbourne Pullman Limited', a Sunday-only all-Pullman service.

Since 1913, Third Class ordinary carriages had been added to nominally all-Pullman services and in 1915 the company took the decisive step of offering Third Class Pullmans. These were older cars, re-configured with fixed seating in four-seat bays on one side of the central aisle and two-seat bays on the other in place of the 1+1 loose armchairs of the First Class fleet. Apart from this slight reduction in comfort, the Third-Class cars were every bit as Pullman as the others, both in style and in service, and a huge improvement on the LBSCR's rather basic provision for the thrifty.

The railways had been placed under Government control from 1914 to support the war effort and by 1918 they were in a weak financial state, facing backlogs of asset maintenance and renewals, staff shortages and sharp increases in costs. The Government seriously considered nationalisation but the eventual decision, enshrined in the 1921 Railways Act, was compulsory grouping of 120 pre-1914 railway companies into four systems with effect from 1st January 1923. The LBSCR and its neighbours were amalgamated into the Southern Railway, an empire that extended from Margate in the east to Padstow in Cornwall.

The Southern Railway was fortunate in having the dynamic and charismatic Sir Herbert Walker as its General Manager. He had been General Manager of the London and South Western Railway (LSWR) and had led the wartime Railway Executive Committee, reporting to the Government. Walker lost no time in welding the Southern's disparate constituent companies into a strong, forward-thinking and customer-focused business. Walker took a pragmatic view of on-board catering arrangements. On-train catering on the former LBSCR and South Eastern routes had been provided by the Pullman company and these arrangements were confirmed and extended. On the other hand, hoteliers Spiers and Pond had run the LSWR's restaurant and 'pantry' cars, evidently to Walker's satisfaction as the Southern renewed their contract for its South Western division and for all of its inter-regional services. Pullman cars were, however, introduced into some 'Ocean Liner Express' services to Southampton.

The 1920s were a period of steady expansion for the Pullman company, which had now established a second stronghold on the London and North Eastern Railway as well as its smaller operations in Scotland and even on the Metropolitan Railway. The Southern Railway laid on a new all-Pullman boat train to Dover that became the 'Golden Arrow' in 1929, when the French Nord company inaugurated a matching luxury service from Calais to Paris. By then, some 60 Pullman cars were operating on the Southern's Central division to Brighton, Worthing, Eastbourne, Newhaven and Hastings.

The Southern Railway announced that an 'entirely new' Southern Belle train would enter service on 1st January 1925 though 'new' merely meant 'different', with a mix of Third Class cars rebuilt from Great War ambulance train stock and First Class cars sourced from stock originally intended for LNER or Southern Railway Eastern Section routes. These included 'Iolanthe', 'Viking' and 'Rosamund', supplemented as required by cars from the 1908 train and even the earlier American cars.

Class H1 'Atlantic' No. 39, designed and built by the LBSCR under the supervision of its Chief Mechanical Engineer, Douglas Earle Marsh, had hauled the 'Southern Belle' on its inaugural run in 1908 and class H1 and H2 Atlantics continued to be used on the service right up to the end of steam haulage, seeming to have no difficulty keeping schedule. From 1914 onwards these Atlantics were supplemented by Lawson Billinton's large, fast and powerful 4-6-4 'Baltic' tank locomotives of class 'L' and from 1926 by the Southern Railway's new 'King Arthur' class 4-6-0s, with their romantic, if historically dubious, names of knights of the Round Table.

In 1928 the Pullman Car Company acquired part of the former LBSCR's workshops and stores at Preston Park, a mile or so north of Brighton station. Here the Company's craftsmen would overhaul, and even on occasion completely rebuild, Pullman cars from all parts of the UK.

LBSCR Class H2 4-4-2 locomotive 424, built in 1911, with a 'Southern Belle' service made up of five of the 1908-1911 Pullman cars. The Pullman Company painted the roofs of their cars white but these quickly weathered to dark grey in the sooty conditions of a steam railway. The still-white roof of the second car suggests that it was 'Vivienne' or 'Myrtle', built in 1911 to supplement the original seven cars in response to the commercial success of the new service. No 424 was designed by D Earle Marsh and was based on the Ivatt 'Atlantics' of the Great Northern Railway. Named 'Beachy Head' by the Southern Railway she had a long and successful career, continuing in service until 1958 on secondary routes between London and the South Coast. *Mike Morant collection*

# Chapter 4
# The Sparks Effect

Twenty-six years earlier, on Sunday 26th July 1903, Driver Thompsett was waiting to depart from Victoria station with the 'Brighton Limited'. He had one of the LBSCR's latest express steam locomotives, B4 4-4-0 no 70 'Holyrood', at the head of just three Pullmans and a Pup and he had been given instructions from on high to make the run in the shortest possible time. Less than 49 minutes later the train was standing at the platform at Brighton, having reached a top speed of 90 miles per hour on the racing straight through Horley.

This frolic had a serious purpose. The LBSCR Board had been galvanised by a proposal to build a new rival non-stop electric line between London and Brighton and were investigating the potential for electric traction on their own main line and the possibility of a 50-minute timing over the 50 miles to Brighton. It had all started with Magnus Volk, a Victorian inventor with a particular interest in electricity. In 1883 he had opened on Brighton seafront one of the world's first electric railways as a curiosity for visitors – it is still operating today. This practical demonstration had helped to spread the idea of electric traction for railways. London's first electric deep level tube line, the City and South London, opened in 1890. Two years later, Leeds became the first city to operate electric trams and a year after that the all-electric Liverpool Overhead Railway opened.

Volk's Electric Railway. Presented to the people of Brighton by Magnus Volk, an inventor and engineer, on August 4th 1883, this narrow gauge railway is now the World's oldest operating public electric railway. It operates along the Brighton seafront from the Aquarium to Black Rock between Easter and September and is well worth a visit. For details, see www.volkselectricrailway.co.uk. The photo shows one of the electric cars on the viaduct at Banjo Groyne in Edwardian days. *Volk's Electric Railway Association*

The LBSCR obtained general powers to electrify its network and commissioned the eminent consulting electrical engineer Philip Dawson to advise the Board. The company's Chief Engineer, Charles Morgan, visited Italy to see the newly-electrified line from Milan to Varese, which used the third-rail system, and the Valtellina main line, electrified on the 3600V a.c. three-phase overhead system. He came down firmly in favour of overhead electrification. Advised by Dawson, the LBSCR contracted with the German firm *Allgemeine Electricitäts Gesellschaft* (AEG) to electrify the South London Line from Victoria to London Bridge via Peckham Rye and Battersea on the overhead system with a 6,600V a.c. 25Hz single phase supply.

In the meantime the London County Council's tramway network in south London, electrified from 1903, was offering a clean, modern, convenient and cheap alternative to the steam suburban railways of south London and particularly to the LBSCR's mean and dingy 4-wheel carriages. The competition hit traffic hard, contibuting to a halving of ticket revenue at some inner suburban stations.

Public operation of the new electric services began on 1st December 1909 and traffic began to recover at once, rising by 50% within the first month and doubling by April 1910. The 'sparks effect', stimulating customer demand by offering fast, frequent, clean and bright electric trains, was working. In the next two years the LBSCR extended its electric network from both Victoria and London Bridge to Crystal Palace and Norwood Junction. The company's subsequent project, a further extension of electrification over most of the LBSCR's suburban lines and including SECR services to Caterham and Tattenham Corner, was halted by World War I, which also, unsurprisingly, terminated the relationship with AEG.

Work resumed on the electrification of routes to Coulsdon North and Sutton in 1922 and was completed by the Southern Railway in 1925. Whereas the earlier schemes had used conventional multiple unit arrangements of power cars and trailers, the Coulsdon and Sutton routes were operated with locomotive vans marshalled between trailers, possibly with a view to the eventual use of electric locomotives to Brighton.

Another Southern constituent, the London and South Western Railway (LSWR), had also been busy electrifying its principal suburban routes. The LSWR used direct current at a nominal 600 Volts, supplied *via* an outside top-contact conductor rail and returned *via* the running rails. It, too, experienced a gratifying surge in traffic as a result.

With these results, the Southern Railway's Board needed no further convincing of the sparks effect. Cleaner, faster, more frequent services attracted traffic that was otherwise being lost to buses and trams. What is more, operating and maintenance costs were far lower, whilst multiple units simplified terminal operations and made more efficient use of track capacity.

But which system to adopt? The company had inherited two different ones and there was a third on the drawing board – 3,000V d.c. four-rail – for the South Eastern and Chatham lines. Of the three, the LSWR's third rail system required the least capital investment per track mile, was the least disruptive to install and represented the largest part of the suburban network already electrified. Accordingly the Southern's Board decided in 1924 that the ex-SECR suburban routes would be electrified on the d.c. third-rail system at 660 Volts and that the ex-LBSCR a.c. overhead routes would be converted to the new standard. By 1929 all of the a.c. equipment had been replaced and one year later the project to electrify virtually all of the Southern's inner-suburban network was complete.

Sir Herbert Walker imposed strict financial targets on each electrification scheme. Projects were carried out as economically as possible. Most of the rolling stock was converted from former steam-hauled or a.c. electric cars and existing semaphore signalling was retained wherever traffic densities did not justify an upgrade. On many stations even the original gas lamps remained in use.

SO SWIFTLY HOME

by

SOUTHERN ELECTRIC

EDMOND VAUGHAN

The Southern strongly promoted its fast, frequent electric train services with posters and booklets extolling the virtues of suburban life, with gratifying financial results for the company. Poster artwork by Edmond Vaughan. *National Railway Museum/Science & Society Picture Library*

An original LSWR 3-car unit heads a suburban electric train at Hounslow, probably in the late 1920s. *Laurie Mack Collection*

# Chapter 5
# 'Gentlemen...'

'Gentlemen, I have decided to electrify to Brighton.' With this startling announcement to the Southern Railway's 1929 Traffic Officers' Conference, Sir Herbert Walker launched Britain's first main line electrification project.

That year the Chancellor, Winston Churchill, had abolished a longstanding tax on First Class fares on condition that the railways used the additional income to fund projects that would help to relieve unemployment. For the Southern, the capitalised future value of the saving was just over £2m. However the Brighton electrification project would cost about £2.7m – about £135m at today's values[3]. To bridge the gap the new electric services would need to generate 6% more revenue in addition to the expected operating cost savings – in fact they were to generate 19% more revenue from increased traffic by the end of the first year[4].

The Southern's project did more than just electrify the Brighton main line: it transformed the scale and quality of the train service. 'Passengers do not like timetables' was one of Walker's aphorisms so the new electric operation, introduced on 1st January 1933, was based on high-frequency services at easy-to-remember regular intervals. The expresses from Victoria to Brighton were the most memorable of all; 'every hour, on the hour, in the hour'.

Including the direct route from Coulsdon North, the limit of the existing suburban electric network, to Brighton, the Quarry Line bypass to the Redhill bottleneck, the lines from Redhill to Reigate and from Preston Park to West Worthing, the Southern electrified over 160 track miles under this scheme. The Central Electricity Board grid delivered power at 33kV a.c. to the railway at three points from which it was cabled to 18 unmanned rectifier substations that supplied 660V d.c. to the third rail, the whole operation being supervised from an electrical control room at Three Bridges.

South of Coulsdon, traffic had been controlled by semaphore signalling using the 'absolute block' principle, whereby only one train could occupy a line between two adjacent manned signal-boxes. As these could be two or more miles apart, the system limited the capacity of the route. The Southern replaced all of the semaphore signalling between Coulsdon and Brighton with semi-automatic three-aspect colour light signals operated by track circuits. With the exceptions of the long Quarry and Clayton tunnels, each of which was a single block section, the new colour light signals were spaced at intervals of between 1,400 and 1,500 yards to accommodate the new, more intensive train service. The company rebuilt Haywards Heath station with two island platforms, remodelled Brighton station to provide longer platforms and to simplify the track layout, and built depots for the new trains at both Brighton and West Worthing.

The Southern decided to use multiple units for the new service, for expresses as well as for local services. There were several reasons for this. First, multiple units eliminate the need to attach and detach locomotives at each end of the journey, freeing track capacity at Victoria, Brighton and London Bridge. The process of lengthening and shortening trains for peak and off-peak traffic levels is similarly simplified and portions of trains can be split and joined to serve two destinations. Second, all of the available platform space at terminals can be used for passenger-carrying vehicles – the 'dead' space for a locomotive at each end is eliminated. Third, multiple unit trains have broadly constant power-to-weight ratios regardless of length so timetabling and performance are standardised. Finally, multiple units have power collection 'shoes' along the length of the train making it easier to cope with the inevitable gaps in the electrified third rail at junctions – potentially a critical factor when accelerating a heavy train through the complex points and crossings outside Victoria station on the steep climb to Grosvenor Bridge.

Whereas most of the Southern's suburban electric multiple units were low-cost rebuilds of old locomotive-hauled coaches, the Brighton line fleets were to be all-new. To this end, during 1932 passengers on the Cobham line caught occasional glimpses of a strange-looking electric train undergoing trials. Unlike the bull-nosed suburban units that were then the mainstay of this route, the powered cars at each end had a well-proportioned but much flatter front with a domed roof. These cars were brand new and resembled the Southern's latest Third Class saloons for main line steam trains. Instead of the usual truss-frame between the bogies these cars had a mysterious collection of equipment boxes instead – Cobham line

---

3   Based on share of GDP – calculated using www.measuringworth.com
4   Dendy Marshall, C. revised by Kidner, R.: 'A History of the Southern Railway'. Ian Allan 1968 p412

One of the Southern Railway's 6-car express electric multiple units built for the launch of the Brighton line electrification on 1st January 1933, seen here near Clapham Junction in 1965. The Pullman car is third in the formation. *Colour-Rail*

passengers were used to such things being tidied away at the back of driving compartments. Between them were marshalled two specially constructed coaches with LSWR bodies, lengthened by new sections to Maunsell profile and mounted on new underframes, and between these an unidentified Maunsell corridor Third. Had they been allowed on board this test train, the passengers would have seen control cabling snaking down the corridors to link the driving motored cars at each end.

Satisfied with the outcome of these trials, the Southern placed orders for its new express electric fleets. The mainstay of the route was to be twenty 6-car units, each consisting of two driving motor brake saloon Thirds flanking four unpowered ('trailer') cars; a compartment Third, two compartment composites and a Pullman car. As with the existing steam-hauled service, the Pullman company would continue to provide on-board catering on all of the new electric expresses. Three more 6-car units, for the 'City Limited' commuter service from Brighton to London Bridge, were generally similar but the three non-Pullman trailers were all First Class. These units are described in more detail in Chapter 20.

As well as these 6-car express units, the Southern built a new fleet of 4-car units for semi-fast and stopping services. These were a superior form of the company's suburban stock, having non-corridor compartments in three cars and a side corridor linking the compartments to two lavatories in the fourth car, though one had to be something of a trainspotter to know which car to travel in if one anticipated the need for relief en route!

No Pullman luxury here but at least the seats were deep and comfortable, One of the 4 LAV units used on Brighton line stopping and semi-fast services is seen here towards the end of its working life heading an 8-car train near Hassocks.
*Michael Baker*

# Chapter 6
# The Electric Belle

The steam-hauled all-Pullman Southern Belle had been a commercial success and had conferred prestige on both organisations so, naturally, both the Southern Railway and the Pullman Car Company wanted the service to continue after electrification of the Brighton Line. The question was, how best to achieve this? Continuing with steam haulage of the existing Pullman cars was both operationally unsatisfactory and risked the Southern Belle appearing old-fashioned alongside the Southern's brand-new 6-car express electric multiple units. And, if new Pullmans were to be built for an electrically-powered Belle, the arguments for multiple unit, rather than electric locomotive, operation were the same as for the Southern's other Brighton expresses.

The two companies agreed to build three all-Pullman electric multiple units – the first such trains in the world – to operate the Southern Belle. The units were similar to the new Brighton line express fleet and had the same running gear, electrical and pneumatic systems, financed and maintained by the Southern Railway. The Southern also provided motormen (the term used to describe electric train drivers) and guards, whilst the Pullman Car Company funded and maintained the car bodies and provided the on-board service to passengers.

The three Belle units each consisted of five cars, all of which were built during 1932 by Metropolitan-Cammell at their Saltley works. Like the motor coaches and the individual Pullmans in the twenty-three 6-car express units, the Belle cars were constructed entirely of steel, something of an innovation as most passenger coaches of the period had a wooden body frame with steel panelling. Each unit was 346ft long, 9ft wide, 12ft 5ins high and weighed 229 tons. Dimensional drawings of the three different types of car are given in Appendix 4.

The two driving motor brake cars both had two 9ft two-axle bogies, each axle having a 225 horsepower (hp) British Thomson-Houston (BTH) type 163 traction motor, suspended from the bogie frame and mounted on the axle by means of a bearing. The motor drove the axle through reduction gears that gave a top speed of about 75mph on level track. Thus, the four powered bogies on the two driving motor brake cars developed a total of 1,800 installed hp.

Each of the motor coach bogies had shoe-beams mounted on both sides to collect electricity from the 660 Volt third rail supply and feed it to a power bus-line running the length of the unit, with jumper cables connecting each car to the next. As well as feeding the traction control equipment on each motor coach, the power bus-line fed a motor-generator set on each of the driving motor brake cars. This delivered a 70 Volt supply for control systems, brake compressors, train lighting and other auxiliary systems. The power bus-line also supplied a dynamotor under the floor of each First Class trailer car that provided a 110 Volt supply for the all-electric kitchen.

Inside each cab was a 'master controller' that enabled the motorman to control the supply of power to the motors in order to regulate the train's speed. The motorman activated ('cut in') the controller in the leading cab by inserting a key. As the motorman moved the handle of the master controller through a quadrant he energised a series of circuits in a multi-core control cable that ran the length of the train and operated the traction control equipment on each power car. The master controller was also known as the 'dead man's handle' because the motorman had to hold it down under spring pressure when driving. If an incapacitated driver released it, the traction current to the motors would be cut and an automatic emergency brake application would be made – a safety feature common to all Southern electric multiple units. The traction control equipment, supplied by Metropolitan-Vickers, consisted of electro-pneumatic contactors that arranged the two motors on each bogie electrically either in series or in parallel and that switched line power through a grid of resistances.

Initially the motors would be connected in series, thereby halving the supply voltage to each motor, and all of the resistances would be connected in series, so reducing the voltage across the motors to a fraction of the line voltage. This was necessary because applying full voltage to a motor that has to overcome the inertia of a stationary train before it can turn would cause a flashover that would severely damage the motor. As the train accelerated the resistances would be progressively switched out until the full line power was being supplied to each pair of in-series motors. These would then be switched to parallel, with all of the resistances back in circuit and the switching-out process would again be carried out until each motor was at full line power. There was a separate reverser control circuit to change the direction of operation of the motors on each power car. Although the Southern's contemporary suburban fleets had contactors that were opened by springs and closed by electro-magnets, on the new Brighton express stock the contactors were, for the first time, operated by compressed air working in cylinders and operating on pistons. Electro-magnets, activated by the 70 Volt control circuits, operated the cylinder air valves.

Because the control equipment on the three Belle units was identical to that on the Southern's six-car Brighton express units, the two fleets could work in multiple with each other and with later builds of pre-war Southern express units. To enable coupled units to be linked electrically, each unit had a single multi-core control jumper cable mounted on the offside and a corresponding receptacle on the nearside. There were no inter-unit power cables but the units did have a receptacle to enable a cable from an overhead power trolley to be connected in order to move them in and out of depots where a third rail would be hazardous.

A characteristic sound of the Southern Electric system was the ringing thump of an electrically operated reciprocating compressor under each motor coach as it periodically topped up the main air reservoir for the Westinghouse automatic air brake. These reservoirs were linked along the train by a 'main air' pipe and also supplied the air for the whistle and the electro-pneumatic contactors that operated the traction control equipment.

When the motorman moved his brake valve to the 'release and running' position, it charged a second 'train brake' pipe with compressed air and this in turn filled auxiliary reservoirs on each coach through a device called a triple valve, which also vented the brake cylinder to atmosphere. When the motorman moved his brake valve to the 'service application' position it allowed air from the train brake pipe to escape to the atmosphere in a controlled manner. The triple valve in each coach sensed this reduction in pressure, closed the feeds from the brake pipe to the auxiliary cylinder and from the brake cylinder to atmosphere and opened a feed from the auxiliary cylinder to the brake cylinder, forcing the piston outwards to operate a mechanical linkage that applied brake blocks to the rim of each wheel. The pressure differential between the train brake pipe and the auxiliary cylinders controlled the strength of the brake application; when the two pressures were again balanced the triple valves would stop feeding air to the brake cylinders.

If the motorman or the guard placed his brake handle in the 'emergency application' position, all of the air in the train brake pipe would be released, slamming on the brakes on

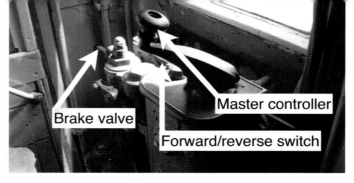

Top: Cab of 11201, part of the Southern Electric Group's preserved pre-war Southern Railway express unit 3142. The electrical control equipment was supplied in 1938 by English Electric but is generally similar to the controls of the Belle units. The master controller, also known as the 'dead man's handle' was spring-loaded and had to be held down quite firmly to prevent the emergency brake applying – motormen needed strong arms! The Forward/Reverse switch is to the left of the master controller lever and the brake valve is to the far left. On the wall to the left of the controls, above the driver's position, were three gauges, an ammeter (top), a speedometer (centre) and a duplex brake pressure gauge (bottom). To the right of the driving position was a handbrake consisting of a pedestal with a vertically mounted rotating handle. *Simon Jeffs*

Above: Driving Motor Brake car, showing third-rail pick-up shoes, and control cables.

all cars. The same would happen if the motorman released the dead-man's handle or if a brake pipe burst, for example because a coupling broke. The passengers and Pullman attendants could also apply the brake by pulling the emergency plunger in each saloon, though in this instance the motorman could 'hold off' the brake so as to avoid stopping in a potentially dangerous place such as a tunnel or a viaduct. When the motorman again placed his brake valve handle in the 'release and running' position, compressed air from the main brake reservoirs was again allowed to enter the train brake pipe. As the pressure in this pipe rose along the train, the triple valve on each coach would exhaust the compressed air in the brake cylinder, producing a series of hissing sighs from the front to the rear of the train, and re-charge the auxiliary cylinder on each coach ready for the next brake application.

# Chapter 7
# Designed for Comfort

Each 5-car Belle unit was made up of two driving motor brake parlour Third Class cars, a trailer parlour Third and two trailer kitchen Firsts, with a total capacity of 40 First Class and 152 Third Class seats. Bodywork was based on contemporary Pullman car design, having a large, rectangular window to each seating bay that incorporated horizontally sliding glazed ventilators and recessed, inwards-opening external passenger doors with deep, oval windows. The units were painted in Pullman umber livery, lined in red and gold, with cream panels between the windows. The Pullman coat of arms was displayed centrally on the front of each driving motor brake car and at both ends of the bodyside of each car.

Pullman practice was to bestow individual names on cars that included First Class accommodation and to prominently display them centrally on the lower bodysides. In keeping with the Belle theme, these and the composite Pullman cars formed in the other Brighton express units were given popular girls' names of the era rather than the traditional Pullman mix of royalty, deities and exotic places. The Third Class cars carried a similarly prominent bodyside legend based on the last two digits of the car's number in the Pullman company's asset schedule, for example 'CAR NO 85 THIRD CLASS', later shortened to 'CAR NO 85'. Each car's full schedule number was displayed on a small cast data plate above the buffers at each end (photo below right).

Each car had pressure ventilation, with fresh air drawn in from outside and passed through a chamber where it was heated electrically in cold weather. To reduce interior noise levels, the floors had cork insulation whilst the majority of the sides and most of the roof area were insulated by thick layers of 'Insulwood', with an air space between each layer.

The motor brake parlour Thirds at each end of each unit consisted of a full width driving cab with inwards opening doors. The cab, which was identical to those in the Southern's other Brighton express units, had a tip-up seat (many motor-men preferred to drive standing) and a pedestal with the master controller and brake valve. These, together with an ammeter, a duplex gauge showing pressures in the main air pipe and the train brake pipe and a speedometer (reputedly never actually connected), were on the left side of the cab as most signals and platforms were on this side.

A separate pedestal was provided on the other side of the cab for the handbrake; the window on this side was hinged on one side to enable the motorman to change the stencil head-code clipped to the outside of the light-box mounted centrally between the cab windows. The Southern had a system of single-character headcodes for its suburban network but adopted double-digit numbers for the Brighton line and subsequent main line electrifications. '4' (with a blank for the second number space) was the designation for Victoria-Brighton or

| 1932 unit no. | 2051 | 2052 | 2053 | Seats | |
|---|---|---|---|---|---|
| 1937 unit no. | 3051 | 3052 | 3053 | 1st | 3rd |
| Driving Motor Brake Parlour Third | Car no. (2)88 | Car no. (2)90 | Car no. (2)92 | | 48 |
| Trailer Kitchen First | (279) 'Hazel' | (284) 'Vera' | (281) 'Gwen' | 20 | |
| Trailer Kitchen First | (282) 'Doris' | (280) 'Audrey' | (283) 'Mona' | 20 | |
| Trailer Parlour Third | Car no. (2)86 | Car no. (2)87 | Car no. (2)85 | | 56 |
| Driving Motor Brake Parlour Third | Car no. (2)89 | Car no. (2)91 | Car no. (2)93 | | 48 |
| | | | TOTAL | 40 | 152 |

The unique external passenger door with its characteristic oval window is seen on Trailer Kitchen First car 'Doris' (formerly in unit 3051) at Horsted Keynes on the Bluebell Railway on 26th June 2009. The car's end gangway has been removed. *Colin Duff*

Left: Third Class car as refurbished in 1968. *Doug Lindsay Collection*

Brighton-Victoria non-stop services and was therefore the usual headcode for the Brighton Belle. The purpose of these headcodes, which were removed at the end of each journey, was to indicate the train's route and stopping pattern to signalmen, although many regular passengers used them to identify 'their' train (see Appendix 2).

There was an internal door on the offside of the cab, leading into a guard's/luggage compartment which had double external doors, one of which opened inwards. A seat and a desk were provided for the guard and a periscope arrangement to roof level so that the guard could view signals – part of the guard's duties in those days was to monitor progress and double-check signals, especially on the approach to junctions. The guard also had a duplex brake pressure gauge and a brake valve for use in an emergency.

As there was no vestibule at the outer end of the passenger saloon, the partition between the guard's compartment and the passenger accommodation incorporated a central emergency exit door. Two 3-bay Third Class saloons ('parlours' in Pullman terminology) had a total of 48 seats arranged 2+2 either side of a central gangway in facing pairs with tables. At the inner end of the car was a passageway with lavatory compartment on one side and two small storage cupboards and a ventilation equipment cupboard on the other. The passageway led into a transverse entrance vestibule with inward opening doors with oval glazing, oval end windows and a corridor connection to the next car. The tare weight of each of these cars was 62 tons and each was 66ft 9ins long.

The cupboard, lavatory and vestibule arrangement was similar at each end of the Trailer Parlour Third, which seated 56 in a four-bay and a three-bay saloon with a central partition. This car weighed 39 tons tare and was 66ft long.

Each unit included two First Class Kitchen Trailers with end vestibules and corridor connections. These flanked a small all-electric kitchen, a pantry and two 2-bay saloons each with eight seats arranged 1+1 either side of a central gangway, a 4-seat coupé and a lavatory. The tare weight of each of these cars was 43 tons, they were 66ft long and were marshalled in a pair with the kitchens at the outer ends.

Interiors were sumptuous and ornate, with subtle Art Deco touches. It is a tradition of Pullman craftsmanship to give each car its own individual decorative character and each of the 15 Belle cars was unique, if only in some small variation in its elaborate hand-crafted marquetry panelling. For example a contemporary account described the interior of 'Doris' as:

'... treated with fine English walnut of three varieties of figures, and the panels are quartered and cross-banded. The decorative effect is obtained by the use of Convex Eagle mirrors, cut in fine boxwood with black beaded rims, and also by the introduction of etchings mounted in black mouldings. The carpets are of rich deep pile in tones of green. The chair

and seat coverings are in moquette velvet, in tones of brown, red and fawn', and 'Gwen' as:

'... the main panel work is in figured English walnut with lace wood and laurel lines. Marquetry work is introduced in the principal panels, and carried out in boxwood, weathered sycamore and red and white natural pear-wood ... the carpet is of Wilton pile, in tones of blue, whilst the chairs are covered in velvet moquette in blue and mauve tints.'[5]

Metalwork was finished in satin silver and each glass-topped table was provided with a classic Pullman table lamp with a tulip-shaped celluloid shade. An electric bell system was linked to a coloured light panel that indicated the location of the call to the attendant. In First Class cars, ceiling lights were enclosed in peach-coloured frosted glass strips whilst in Third Class the effect of the semi-recessed ceiling bulbs was softened by down-lighters on side and end panels.

---

5  *The Locomotive*, 14 January 1933, quoted in Charles Fryer; 'British Pullman Trains', Silver Link Publishing, 1992.

First Class car 'Gwen', probably in late pre-war or early post-war days. Opposite: First Class car 'Vera' in original condition. *Doug Lindsay Collection*

First Class car 'Audrey' in original condition. *Doug Lindsay Collection*

Opposite: First Class car 'Doris' in original 1933 condition. *Doug Lindsay Collection*

Third Class car no. 87 in original condition. *Doug Lindsay Collection*

Opposite top: One of the two saloons of First Class car 'Doris' *Colin Duff*

Opposite centre: The glass diffusers over the parlour car ceiling lights were decorated with an art-deco sunburst pattern. *Simon Jeffs, artefact from the collection of Anthony Ford*

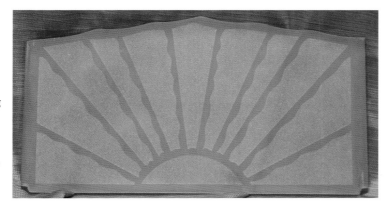

Above: This pattern was repeated on the downlighters from Third Class cars. *Simon Jeffs (photo), artefact from the collection of Anthony Ford*

Right: ... and even the door handles. *Simon Jeffs (photo), artefact from the collection of Anthony Ford*

Upper far right: The iconic Pullman lamp with tulip-shaped shade. *Simon Jeffs (photo), artefact from the collection of Anthony Ford*

Far right: Each lamp was allocated to an individual car, and was identified with a stamp on the base. The example shown is from 'Audrey'. *Simon Jeffs (photo), artefact from the collection of Anthony Ford*

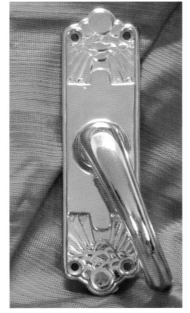

Opposite: The BEL units were the only Southern Electric multiple units to carry a clock. *Colin Duff*

Right: Each seat was numbered. *Colin Duff*

Far right: The bell to summon the attendant was set in the car wall. *Colin Duff*

# Chapter 8
# The Belle Enters Service

Electrification, with its frequent services and high quality rolling stock, provided a much-needed economic boost to Brighton and its neighbours and the Mayor of Brighton, Councillor Frank G. Beal, J.P., congratulated the Southern Railway '... on their vision and enterprise and the South Coast resorts upon the new asset of incalculable value which the Company had presented to them as a New Year's gift'.

The new Brighton line timetable, launched on Sunday 1st January 1933, had an express service each hour throughout the day. Of these, the 11.00am, 3.00pm and 7.00pm departures

from Victoria and the 1.25pm, 5.25pm and 9.25pm return departures were Southern Belle all-Pullman services. All were non-stop and shown in the public timetable as completing the journey in exactly 60 minutes – the working timetable generally had the services arriving a minute or two earlier. Two of the three units were kept overnight under cover in the station platforms at Victoria and taken out to the Battersea Pier carriage sidings every weekday morning to get them out of the way of the peak commuter traffic, after which they returned to the station in good time for the 11.00am Brighton service.

New and old at Victoria. On 1st January 1933 the inaugural 'Southern Belle' waits to depart from Victoria station whilst a 30-year-old ex-LSWR Drummond S11 heads a train over the yet to be electrified Mid-Sussex route. *National Railway Museum*

Once the 11.00am service had arrived at Brighton, the pair of units ran empty to the Southern's electric multiple unit depot at Lovers' Walk, where they were split. One unit remained at the depot for maintenance whilst the other returned to the station to work the 1.25pm service to Victoria solo. On returning from Victoria at 4.00pm, it was coupled to the previous day's maintenance unit for the 5.25pm run back up to town. On arrival at Victoria, the two units split again. One unit shunted back to the carriage sidings to get out of the way for the evening peak, returning later to the platforms to stable overnight. The other operated the 7.00pm service to Brighton, returning to Victoria at 9.25pm to be re-united with the first unit and stabled overnight in the platform at Victoria. However these arrangements were flexible and adjusted according to anticipated loadings and the spare unit was often kept at Streatham Hill depot in south London.

As with locomotive hauled Pullman cars, the Southern Railway was responsible for operations and for maintaining the underframes, bogies and traction equipment of the 5-car Belle units. The bodies and interior fittings were maintained by Pullman at its works at Preston Park, Brighton, set up in 1928 in part of the former LBSCR's workshops and stores. The two units that were normally in traffic rotated with a third that was held spare or undergoing routine maintenance at Lovers' Walk, which dealt with one unit per day from Monday to Saturday. The Belle units would also occasionally visit the Southern's depot at Peckham Rye for major overhauls to running gear and electrical equipment and for repairs that could not be undertaken at Lovers' Walk.

From 1931, when the all-Pullman 'Bournemouth Belle' had started running, the 'Southern Belle' was no longer the only Belle on the Southern Railway. Accordingly, in a ceremony at Brighton station on 29th June 1934, the then Lady Mayor of Brighton, Miss M. Hardy, renamed the service the 'Brighton Belle', a title that the train would carry for the rest of its life. At Victoria station, platform 17, normally dedicated to the Belle service, was given a decorative 'Brighton Belle' arch over the entrance from the concourse.

There were more celebrations on 29th June 1934 when the 'Southern Belle' was renamed the 'Brighton Belle'.

Electrification of the Brighton main line had been a huge financial success and, despite the difficult economic times, the Southern's Chairman, Sir Herbert Walker, persuaded the Board to electrify the line from Haywards Heath (Keymer Junction) to Eastbourne and onwards to Hastings, a project that was completed in July 1935. For this extension the Southern Railway procured 17 more 6-car electric express units to augment its existing 23-strong fleet.

As before, the on-board catering on the Eastbourne route would be in the hands of the Pullman Car Company. However, financing 15 new cars for the Brighton Belle and a further 23 for the other express units of the 1933 scheme had so over-stretched the Pullman company's finances that it had had to negotiate deferred payments with the builders, Metropolitan-Cammell. This time the Southern Railway agreed to provide the catering facilities on the new fleet, which simply consisted of a pantry (kitchenette) and counter, staffed by a Pullman steward and providing a limited range of light refreshments.

Until these new units joined the fleet, the three Brighton Belle units had been designated '5 PUL' in operating publications and the 6 car units with a single Pullman car were coded '6 COR' or '6 COR*' (see Chapter 20). To distinguish the two 6-car fleets the 6 COR units were recoded to '6 PUL', the new fleet was described as '6 PAN' and the Brighton Belle all-Pullman units became '5 BEL'. The 6-car fleets were pooled in order to provide Pullman cars on Brighton, Eastbourne and Worthing routes and '6 PUL/6 PAN' became the standard formation for the majority of 12-car trains.

The Brighton Belle fleet underwent a further change of identity at the beginning of 1937. As the range of unit numbers for suburban electrics (1201-1999) was becoming overcrowded, the number series 2001-2999 was assigned to fleets that were intended primarily for main-line stopping services but were technically compatible with the suburban fleets. To make room, existing gangwayed express units (which could not operate in multiple with suburban-type units) were renumbered in the 3001-3999 series and the three Brighton Belle units accordingly changed from 2051-2053 to 3051-3053.

The formal re-christening was carried out by Miss M. Hardy, Brighton's Mayor at the time, when the Belle arrived from Victoria at noon on 29th June. The coat of arms of Brighton is displayed on the front of the unit. An art deco poster was commissioned from a leading poster designer. *National Railway Museum/SSPL*

# THE BRIGHTON BELLE'S ROUTE

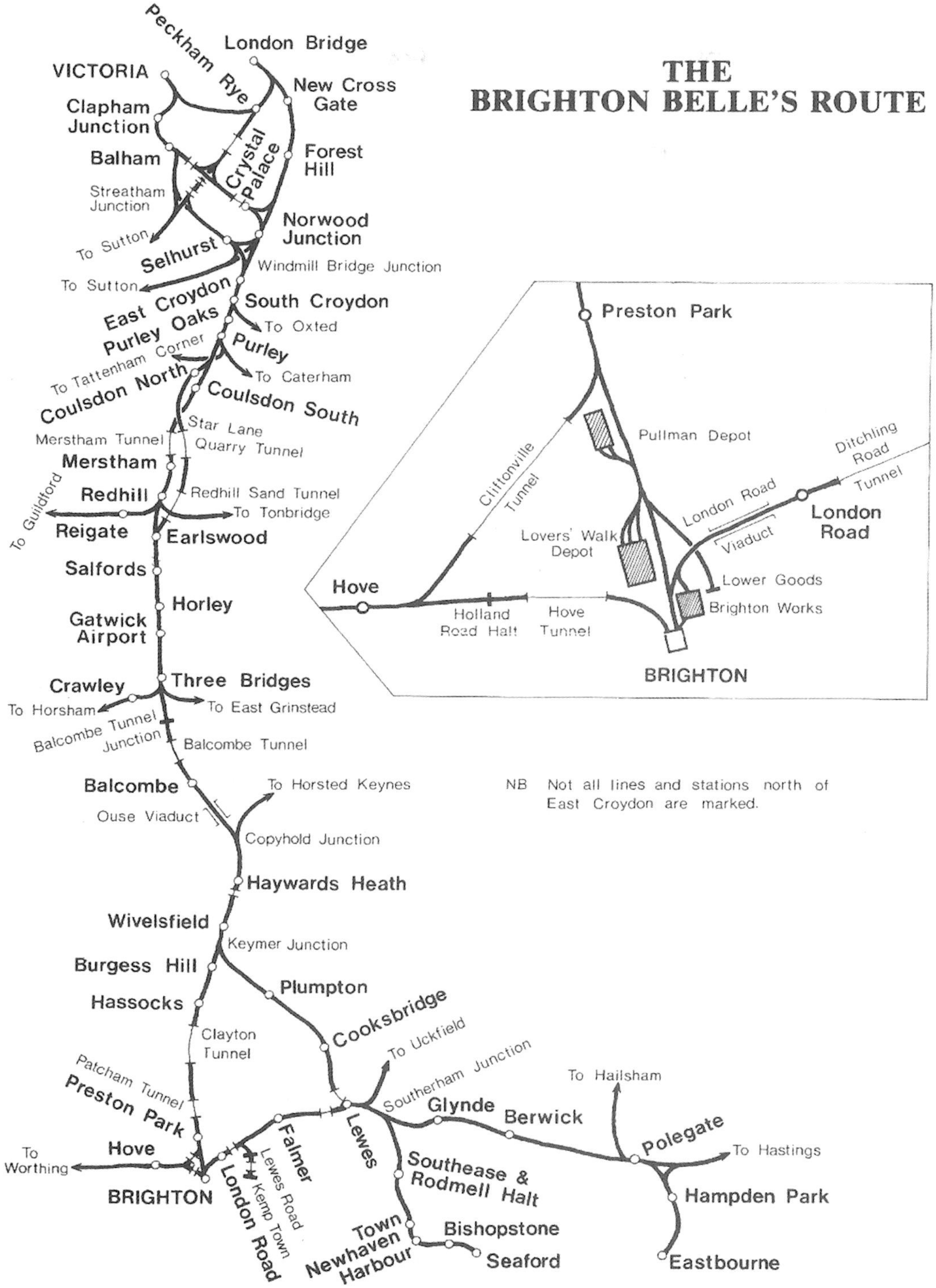

London Bridge
Peckham Rye
VICTORIA
New Cross Gate
Clapham Junction
Forest Hill
Crystal Palace
Balham
Streatham Junction
Norwood Junction
To Sutton
Selhurst
Windmill Bridge Junction
To Sutton
East Croydon
South Croydon
Purley Oaks
To Oxted
Tattenham Corner
Purley
To Tattenham
Coulsdon North
Coulsdon South
To Caterham
Star Lane
Merstham Tunnel
Quarry Tunnel
Merstham
Redhill
Redhill Sand Tunnel
To Guildford
Reigate
To Tonbridge
Earlswood
Salfords
Horley
Gatwick Airport
Crawley
Three Bridges
To Horsham
To East Grinstead
Balcombe Tunnel Junction
Balcombe Tunnel
Balcombe
To Horsted Keynes
Ouse Viaduct
Copyhold Junction
Haywards Heath
Wivelsfield
Keymer Junction
Burgess Hill
Hassocks
Plumpton
Clayton Tunnel
Cooksbridge
To Uckfield
Patcham Tunnel
Southerham Junction
Preston Park
Glynde
Berwick
To Hailsham
Hove
Lewes
Polegate
To Worthing
BRIGHTON
Falmer
Lewes Road
Kemp Town
London Road
Southease & Rodmell Halt
To Hastings
Hampden Park
Town
Newhaven
Harbour
Bishopstone
Seaford
Eastbourne

## Brighton inset

Preston Park
Clittonville Tunnel
Pullman Depot
Ditchling Road Tunnel
London Road
London Road
Viaduct
Lovers' Walk Depot
Lower Goods
Hove
Holland Road Halt
Hove Tunnel
Brighton Works
BRIGHTON

NB  Not all lines and stations north of East Croydon are marked.

The Brighton main line, showing electrified routes from London Bridge and Victoria to Brighton, Seaford and Eastbourne. The Brighton Belle always ran from Victoria (except for rare diversions, when London Bridge became the terminus) via Clapham Junction, Norbury, East Croydon, the Quarry Line (the fast lines avoiding Redhill), Haywards Heath and Hassocks. The Eastbourne Pullman branched off at Keymer Junction to head for Eastbourne via Lewes and Polegate. All the main lines depicted remain open in 2011, with the exception of the 'Cuckoo Line' from Polegate to Hailsham and Eridge and the Lewes-Uckfield line. The branch from Copyhold Junction runs as afar as Ardingly for aggregates traffic. The Bluebell Railway has aspirations to reopen this branch from Horsted Keynes.

The 'Brighton Belle' arch over the entrance to Platform 17 at Victoria station in the 1960s. *Transport Trust Collection*

The popularity of the Belle was such that postcards became widely available. The painting of unit 2051 is remarkably accurate. This particular example came from Michael Baker's collection and was posted on 24th June 1936 from Croydon and was addressed 'My dear Ron' in Worthing from Mummy and tells him that 'the linet (sic) at the shaw is very busy feeding the young ones. Daddy found a wasp's nest under the roof of the porch there and had to destroy it'. *Southern Electric Group archives*

A motor coach from unit 3052 is overhauled at Preston Park Pullman Works in the summer of 1955. Note the open left-hand windscreen. This was hinged to enable the motorman to change the headcode stencil on the opaque panel between the two windows. The driving position was on the left, and only this window had a windscreen wiper. *J J Smith Collection*

# Chapter 9
# A Trip to Brighton – 1936

Let us take a trip to Brighton. Shortly before 11am on a week-day morning in the late summer of 1936, we make our way over the crowded concourse of London's Victoria station to platform 17. After showing our Third Class tickets at the barrier, which is surmounted by a decorative 'Brighton Belle' arch, we walk to the front of the 10-car Pullman train and buy our supplement from the attendant at the door, who invites us to sit where we like as it will not be very busy today.

Passing through the vestibule with its oval windows and turning left through the narrow passageway, we enter a saloon with groups of four seats, each with its own table adorned by a silver Art Deco lamp and covered with a crisp, white table-cloth already laid for morning coffee. Squeezing into the seats – they are a bit tight and the armrests do not help – we look around at the interior. Even in Third Class, each car has its own decorative style, though less elaborate than those of the First Class cars. In this one, the designer has wholeheartedly embraced the latest trends, with wall panelling enlivened by marquetry sunbursts in contrasting Empire hardwoods, satin silver luggage racks, ceiling strip-lights and the seats trimmed in a strident 'jazz' pattern moquette.

As the clock over the doorway at the end of the saloon shows 11.00 the train moves off. We notice how effective the sound insulation is as she glides slowly over the complex pointwork of the station throat. On the South Eastern lines over to our left, another Pullman train – the 'Golden Arrow' – is departing for Dover, its olive-green 'Lord Nelson' class steam locomotive making heavy weather of the short, sharp climb to Grosvenor Bridge over the Thames. No such problems for us, with 3,600 horsepower and 16 driven axles for our 10-car train we soon leave the 'Golden Arrow' struggling in our wake. A brief glimpse of the 'Temple of Power', Sir Giles Gilbert-Scott's impressive new Battersea power station with its two smoking chimneys, then a long, right-hand downward swoop past the soot-blackened terraced houses of Battersea before we again turn towards the south beyond Clapham Junction.

As London's slums give way to elegant, spacious Victorian and Edwardian villas we reflect that it was the railway that made it possible for well-to-do families and their servants to move out to the health-giving fresh air of the suburbs whilst father commuted by steam train to his office in the City. Those trains are electric now; faster, cleaner and more frequent, and

what had once been open fields beyond London are rapidly being developed with huge new estates of semi-detached houses for clerks, typists and shop-workers. New factories on modern suburban industrial estates are producing consumer goods such as radios, vacuum cleaners and washing machines that will be powered by electricity from the new National Grid. Arterial roads link the new developments and more and more middle-class families are buying their first car. There are no rail links to those new factories and the companies' fleets of road vans transport their goods to the warehouses and shops.

It is an age of transport wonders. Electric trains may no longer be a novelty but an electric Pullman express certainly is. The giant new Cunard liner 'Queen Mary' has just won the Blue Riband with the first westbound crossing of the Atlantic in just under four days. Imperial Airways is operating from Croydon Aerodrome to destinations in Africa and India and has now linked with the newly-formed QANTAS airline to provide a through service from London to Brisbane in just twelve days.

Our musings are abruptly ended by a series of shuddering crashes as the heavy motor bogies of our leading Pullman car negotiate Coulsdon North Junction where the slow Brighton lines diverge from ours to take the 'old' route via Redhill. The attendant, who knew what was coming, had braced himself against our table as he deftly poured our fresh coffee but, as we plunge into the darkness of the Cane Hill covered way in the grounds of the large asylum on the slopes of the Coulsdon hills, wavelets of coffee transfer themselves from cups to saucers and so back to the Pullman Company via the tablecloth.

Now we are on the so-called 'Quarry' line, which is part of the continuous four-track railway completed in 1911 from Victoria to Balcombe Tunnel Junction. Plans were drawn up to extend quadrupling on to Brighton, but the costs of extra tunnels through the South Downs were deemed too great, and the line south of Three Bridges remains a bottleneck. The Quarry line crosses over the slow line at Star Lane, then takes a more easterly course. A deep chalk cutting heralds our approach to Quarry Tunnel and we emerge to glimpse Merstham station to our right which only serves the slow lines. Whilst building the Quarry Line, the LBSCR received a request from the eccentric owner of Hooley Court, who wished the railway to paint all the telegraph poles within sight of his house green and to affix Union Jack flags atop each! His request was officially 'mislaid'.

The Holmethorpe Works of British Industrial Sand give their name to the short Sand Tunnel, where the South Eastern Railway line to Tonbridge and on to Dover passes over us. This was part of the first route from London to Dover, bypassed in 1868 when the Sevenoaks cut-off was opened. The only boat trains down our line connect with the ferries sailing between Newhaven and Dieppe.

Our route again runs parallel with the slow lines for the almost straight, gently descending racing stretch from Earlswood to Three Bridges. We are on time so our driver holds the speed below the official maximum of 75mph but even so the ride is lively. Salfords station on our right was originally a private halt for workers at the adjacent Monotype printing equipment factory but was opened to the public with the extension of electrification to Three Bridges in 1932. The large station at Horley, similar in style to those between East Croydon and Balham and dating from the quadrupling of 1905, passes in a flash, followed in quick succession by the now-closed Gatwick Racecourse station and the newly-opened Gatwick Airport station, linked by a footbridge to the brand-new, avant-garde 'Beehive' air terminal with a solitary de Havilland DH84 biplane outside. Will Gatwick ever replace Croydon as London's main airport, we wonder?

Another series of lurches and thumps from the equalising beams of the bogies and we are through Three Bridges. Turning our attention from the scene outside to our morning papers and the world seems an increasingly threatening place. Under Mussolini's dictatorship, Italy has completed its annexation of Abyssinia, showing the League of Nations to be impotent. In Spain, General Franco is mounting a military *coup d'etat* against the newly-elected left-wing government and civil war seems likely. The Foreign Secretary, Neville Chamberlain, is urging 'restraint' as Hitler's Germany consolidates its reoccupation of the Rhineland by building extensive fortifications. What is not in the newspapers, though it is widely publicised in America with much speculation about the relationship, is any mention of King Edward VIII's Mediterranean yachting cruise in the company of Mrs Wallis Simpson. Monarchs, it seems, no longer conduct their amorous affairs in Brighton.

We note that the countryside passing our window is changing in character, the chalk of the North Downs and flat farmland of the Weald giving way to the sandstone ridge of the Ardingly beds and the High Weald of Sussex. The trees of St Leonard's Forest close in on both sides, four lines become two and we plunge into the long and damp Balcombe Tunnel.

Unit 3053 approaches Merstham on the Quarry Line in 1937. This location was frequently used for publicity shots of the new Brighton electric expresses. *Lens of Sutton*

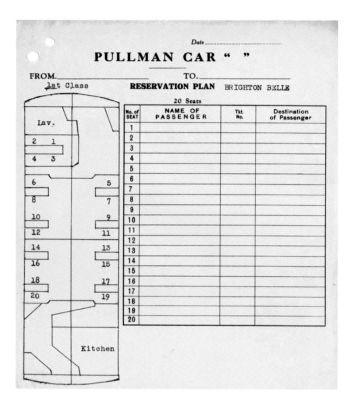

PULLMAN CAR " "

FROM.      TO.
1st Class      **RESERVATION PLAN** BRIGHTON BELLE

20 Seats

| No. of SEAT | NAME OF PASSENGER | Tkt. No. | Destination of Passenger |
|---|---|---|---|
| 1 | | | |
| 2 | | | |
| 3 | | | |
| 4 | | | |
| 5 | | | |
| 6 | | | |
| 7 | | | |
| 8 | | | |
| 9 | | | |
| 10 | | | |
| 11 | | | |
| 12 | | | |
| 13 | | | |
| 14 | | | |
| 15 | | | |
| 16 | | | |
| 17 | | | |
| 18 | | | |
| 19 | | | |
| 20 | | | |

PULLMAN CAR " "

FROM.      TO.
SEAT Nos. 1 - 48   **RESERVATION PLAN** BRIGHTON BELLE
3rd Class

| No. of SEAT | NAME OF PASSENGER | Tkt No | Destination of Passenger |
|---|---|---|---|

More paperwork! First and Third Class seat reservations cards for the Belle's attendants. *Simon Jeffs (photo) from the Anthony Ford Collection*

Over our heads, the nascent tributaries of the River Mole drip through the porous sandstone, causing so much trouble to the electrics in the tunnel that it is lined with lead.

Shaking off a few droplets of water, the Belle is now in glorious Sussex countryside. The quaint, country station of Balcombe comes and goes and then we are on the major engineering feature of the line, the Ouse Viaduct. Described as 'one of the most magnificent undertakings ever constructed' at the time of its completion, it is 462 yards long, up to 100 feet high and supported on 37 arches. The balustrades are of Caen stone and there are two small classical villas at each end, four in all. Below can be seen the tiny stream that will eventually reach the sea at Newhaven as the River Ouse. To the left are the red brick buildings of Ardingly College and to the right, over a sea of oak trees, is the Nymans Estate. Our coffee cups pause in mid-air as we drink in this scene of perfect rural Englishness.

Up and Down loops appear, to serve the four platforms of the busy commuter railhead of Haywards Heath, then after a short tunnel, we are the last leg of our journey to Brighton. Our plates are collected and the bill requested as we pass through the quaint station named Wivelsfield (actually in the Burgess Hill suburb of World's End, but this wasn't thought to be a particularly suitable name for a station!) where the line

to Newhaven, Eastbourne and Ore diverges, then Burgess Hill and Hassocks.

Ahead is the looming mass of the South Downs and what appears to be the entrance to a castle. This is quickly revealed as the north portal of Clayton Tunnel, the longest on the line at 2259 yards and built in a flamboyant crenellated style, complete with cottage between the two turrets. Clayton Tunnel's other claim to fame is more sombre as it was the scene of a dreadful accident on Sunday 25th August 1861 when two trains collided inside the tunnel with the loss of 23 lives. The fault lay with the primitive signalling then in force and led to improvements in procedures and technology that continue to this day, making rail travel a very safe mode of transport. The line descends through a deep cutting, then, after one more short tunnel at Patcham, we enter the suburbs of Brighton.

Our attendant discreetly brings our attention to payment of our bill as the Belle slows through Preston Park station where the line to Worthing and Littlehampton diverges to our right. Brighton is a major railway centre and we pass on our right the Pullman Company works and the servicing depot at Lovers' Walk, while to our left is the Brighton Works, constructing and maintaining many of the Southern Railway's steam locomotives.

The Brighton Belle waits to return to London. The BR Standard tank locomotive in the background provides one of the few clues that this view was taken much later than 1936. *Michael Baker*

As the train glides to a halt under the echoing roof of Brighton station we ease ourselves out of our seats, recover our possessions, bid farewell to our attendant and step down on to the platform. Since electrification Brighton has become one of the busiest stations in the British Isles, with frequent services to London and all points west and east along the Sussex coast, plus country routes to Horsham via Shoreham and Steyning and Tunbridge Wells via Lewes and Uckfield as well as the short, steep branch line to Devil's Dyke, though Brighton's other suburban route to Kemp Town closed when the new main line electric service was inaugurated in January 1933.

However, our journey is over and as we emerge on to Queen Street, we can see right down the hill to the sea, sparkling in the sunshine. For all the criticism it received at the time, there is no doubt that Rennie picked an excellent spot for his station although the long toil up the hill for the return journey as the minutes ticked away before one's train departed has doubtless tried generations of weary families!

Meanwhile, the Belle is prepared for its return journey to London and waits to receive another trainload of passengers to convey to the capital.

# Chapter 10
# War and Peace

On the outbreak of war with Germany in September 1939, the Government placed the railways under the control of the Ministry of Transport, who appointed a Railway Executive Committee to manage them in support of the war effort. Initially the train service was drastically reduced and all Pullman and other catering services were withdrawn but, as the 'phoney war' progressed, this appeared to be an over-reaction and some Pullman services, including Brighton Belle workings, were reinstated on 1st January 1940. Usually a single 5 BEL unit worked in tandem with a 6 PUL or 6 PAN unit to provide both Pullman and non-Pullman accommodation.

However, in September 1940 the 'blitz' on London that was to last to May 1941 began in earnest. At 10.25pm on 9th October 1940, high-explosive bombs fell through the roof of Victoria station where Brighton Belle stock was berthed

as usual at Platform 17. Here, 5 BEL unit 3052 was badly knocked about, car 91 being reported as the most seriously damaged. 3052 was removed to the large and under-utilised Crystal Palace (High Level) station where it was stored under tarpaulins for the duration.

Pullman and other catering services were again withdrawn from May 1942 and units 3051 and 3053 were then also stored. Pullman and other catering services were restored in May 1946 but it was not until 7th October of that year that a Belle unit, 3051, re-entered traffic. 3051 ran for a short time as a six-car unit with trailers 'Doris', 'Hazel', 'Mona' and 'Gwen' until 3053 re-joined the fleet the following month.

*Pullman car 'Audrey' was badly damaged in the raid on Victoria on the 9th October 1940. Workmen clear-up in the aftermath.*
*Kevin Robertson Collection*

After the war, damaged unit 3052 was sent to Metropolitan-Cammell for structural repair and then to the Pullman workshops at Preston Park for refurbishment. In the course of this work, the two motor coaches were marshalled at opposite ends to the unit's pre-war formation. Such was the acute post-war shortage of steel and other supplies that 3052 was not returned to service until September 1947. In the meantime the two available 5 BEL units alternated daily between operating and maintenance spare and at peak times the 5 BEL unit was paired with a 6 PUL unit to provide the necessary capacity.

Belle advertising 1. Reminiscent of the 'Four Belles' poster from the late 1940s that advertised the Devon, Bournemouth, Brighton and Kentish Belles 'ringing the coast', this 1959 advertisement promotes the Southern's two surviving services. The emphasis is on service, with a smiling attendant offering a Pullman car.
*Anthony Ford Collection*

A Labour government had been returned to power in 1945 with a mandate to nationalise the railway companies as part of a wider strategy to bring passenger and freight transport under State control. From 1st January 1948 the Southern Railway became the Southern Region of British Railways (BR). The Southern's contracts with Frederick Hotels Ltd and Bertram & Company Ltd for station and restaurant car catering were terminated over the next couple of years but the Pullman contract had several years to run so, in the short term, the company was not affected by the Southern's change of ownership. However in 1954 British Railways' parent, the British Transport Commission (BTC), acquired the Ordinary share capital of the Pullman Car Company and with it effective control of the business. From then, Pullman was part of the BTC Hotels Executive, the entity that ran station refreshment rooms and the catering on BR's restaurant cars.

Between 1948 and 1957, one of the three 5 BEL units operated a Sunday round trip to Eastbourne – an echo of the 1908 'Eastbourne Pullman Limited'. The train left Victoria at 10.40am, arrived at Eastbourne at 12.00 noon and returned at 5.45pm. Apart from this, and occasional use on Royal and VIP specials, the three units continued to work essentially the same daily Brighton Belle schedule throughout the 1950s and early 1960s. The three units were generally refurbished by Pullman in 1955 (3051 and 3052) and 1956 (3053).

The BTC was abolished in 1962 and British Railways was restructured as a business under the chairmanship of Dr Richard Beeching, with a mandate to return the railways to profitability. Ownership of Pullman Car Company passed from the BTC's disbanded Hotels Executive and became part of BR's Hotels & Catering Services. Perhaps as a result of this change of ownership, BR decided to increase the utilisation of the Brighton Belle fleet by operating an extra daily round trip with effect from the September 1963 timetable change. The new schedule included a late evening post-theatre service that left Victoria at 11.00pm and called additionally at Haywards Heath. The new schedule had the effect of moving the units' base to Brighton and timings became:

9.40am Brighton-Victoria
11.00am Victoria-Brighton
1.25pm Brighton-Victoria (not Sunday)
3.00pm Victoria-Brighton (not Sunday)
5.25pm Brighton-Victoria
7.00pm Victoria-Brighton
8.25pm Brighton-Victoria (not Sunday)
11.00pm Victoria-Brighton (not Sunday).

On Fridays, the 11.00am service attached to a second unit on arrival at Brighton and the Belle ran as a 10-car train for the rest of the day and all day on Saturday and Sunday.

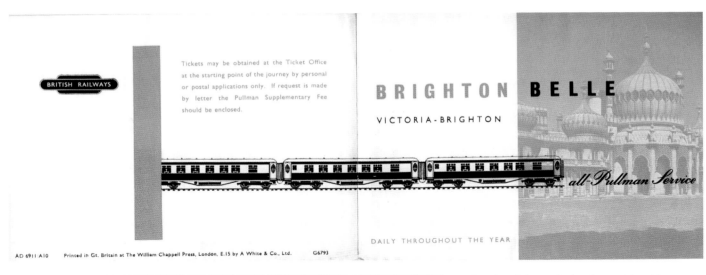

Belle advertising 2. Dating from 1961, this brochure shows the same somewhat-stylised Pullman cars as the 1959 advertisement, here apparently heading into the Brighton Pavilion. *Anthony Ford Collection*

FROM SEPTEMBER 9

NEW
2
ALL-PULLMAN LUXURY

BRIGHTON BELLES

British Railways
SOUTHERN REGION

AD9667/A25/21863

Opposite: A remarkable advert from 1966 depicting a 'cutaway' view of what is apparently a First-Class 5 BEL Trailer, accurately showing the 16-seat Parlour, 4-seat coupe compartment, pantry and kitchen. This should be compared to the photos of 'Doris' in Chapter 7. *Anthony Ford Collection*

The extra services in 1963 were advertised with a stylish (very Hardy Amies fashions) day and night theme. Passengers ('executives and housewives' – the idea of female executives was apparently not considered in 1963) were urged to travel to town on the 9.40am from Brighton and return on the 11.00pm after a West End show. Supper could be enjoyed on the late train stabled at platform 17 from 10.00pm, and inclusive First- or Second-Class packages including up travel on the 9.0am, 1.25pm or 5.25pm, Pullman supplements and supper on the 11.00pm down, were available. *Anthony Ford Collection*

LAVATORY        COUPE COMPARTMENT                              1ST CLASS SALOON

# THE BRIGHTON BELLE / THE BOURNEMOUTH BELLE

all **PULL**...

● Return fares are double the single fares

| | WEEKDAYS | | | | SUNDAYS | | SINGLE FARES |
|---|---|---|---|---|---|---|---|
| VICTORIA dep. | 11 00 | 15 00 | 19 00 | 23 00 | 11 00 | 19 00 | |
| BRIGHTON arr. | 12 00 | 16 00 | 20 00 | 00 02 | 12 00 | 20 00 | VICTORIA/BRIGHTON |
| BRIGHTON dep. | 09 25 | 13 25 | 17 25 | 20 25 | 09 25 17 25 | 20 25 | 1st CLASS 20/9 |
| VICTORIA arr. | 10 25 | 14 25 | 18 25 | 21 25 | 10 25 18 25 | 21 25 | 2nd CLASS 14/- |

**Brighton**

● Fares are liable to alteration

● Return...

| | DAILY | |
|---|---|---|
| WATERLOO dep. | 12 30 | |
| SOUTHAMPTON CTL. arr. | 14 03 | WATER... |
| BOURNEMOUTH CTL. arr. | 14a45 | 1st CLA... |
| | | WATER... |
| | | 1st CLA... |
| BOURNEMOUTH CTL. dep. | 16 36 | |
| SOUTHAMPTON CTL. dep. | 17 15 | |
| WATERLOO arr. | 18 53 | |

**Bournemouth**

a-On Saturdays from 18th Ju...

---

1ST CLASS SALOON                          PANTRY          KITCHEN

# E BOURNEMOUTH BELLE

all **PULLMAN** luxury — all the year round

...fares are double the single fares

| SINGLE FARES |
|---|
| VICTORIA/BRIGHTON |
| 1st CLASS 20/9 |
| 2nd CLASS 14/- |

**Brighton**

● Fares are liable to alteration

● Return fares are double the single fares

| | DAILY | SINGLE FARES |
|---|---|---|
| WATERLOO dep. | 12 30 | |
| SOUTHAMPTON CTL. arr. | 14 03 | |
| BOURNEMOUTH CTL. arr. | 14a45 | WATERLOO/SOUTHAMPTON CTL. |
| | | 1st CLASS £1.12.6  2nd CLASS £1.1.9 |
| | | WATERLOO/BOURNEMOUTH CTL. |
| BOURNEMOUTH CTL. dep. | 16 36 | 1st CLASS £2.4.0  2nd CLASS £1.9.3 |
| SOUTHAMPTON CTL. dep. | 17 15 | |
| WATERLOO arr. | 18 53 | |

**Bournemouth**

a-On Saturdays from 18th June, 1966, arrive three minutes later.

● PULLMAN CAR SUPPLEMENTARY FEES

| | 1st CLASS | 2nd CLASS |
|---|---|---|
| VICTORIA/BRIGHTON | 4/- | 2/6 |
| WATERLOO/SOUTHAMPTON | 6/6 | 4/- |
| WATERLOO/BOURNEMOUTH | 8/- | 6/- |

● Tickets may be obtained at the ticket office at the starting point of the journey by personal or postal application only. If request is made by letter the Pullman supplementary fee should be enclosed.

# Chapter 11
# Belle Life

Throughout its independent existence the Pullman Car Company Ltd had been a small but profitable business. Its success was built on consistently high standards of service delivered by a tightly-knit organisation with short lines of communication from top to bottom. Its head office was a modest suite of rooms above Platform 2 at Victoria station, top management knew the key on-board staff personally and the company's inspectors kept an effective grip on day-to-day operations.

A Pullman crew consisted of a conductor who was in overall charge of the service on board the train, a chef for each kitchen and teams of attendants, each under the supervision of a leading attendant. According to Julian Morel, a former Pullman catering manager[6], many of the best Pullman chefs came from the Services where they were accustomed to working in a confined space, were clean, knew how to improvise and were well disciplined. Recruits from hotels, used to large kitchens and to focusing on one job at a time, found the task of single-handedly preparing a large number of meals from a tiny, swaying kitchen extremely demanding and many left after a short time.

The essence of Pullman catering was simple fare, using the best ingredients and served with style. Main meals might include soup or fruit juice followed by Dover sole or steak with French fried potatoes, eggs and bacon or a salad. The meal was rounded off with coffee, cheese and biscuits. Alternatively customers could opt for something lighter – a round of smoked salmon sandwiches with a pot of tea and a toasted teacake, perhaps. Champagne, wine, spirits, cigarettes and cigars were, of course, all on offer.

Presentation was a key element of the Pullman magic. Tables, each with the signature shaded lamp, were laid with crisp, white cloths and gleaming, polished silverware. Meals and snacks were served on good quality crockery by a smartly-dressed attendant (never 'steward' and certainly not 'waiter'!). Before the war, attendants were dressed in a dark blue three-piece uniform with a cap. In the post-war period the jacket was replaced by a white shell-type jacket with blue trimmings. Leading attendants were identified by blue shoulder cords and the conductor by gold cords.

---

6    Morel, J.: 'Pullman'. David & Charles 1983 p148-170

Prior to the 1963 timetable change, one Pullman crew would staff all three Brighton Belle round trips on a normal weekday – there was no changeover part-way through the day. It was hard work, starting with loading and stowing stores. Most of these had been sent up by van from the Pullman depot that backed on to Stewarts Lane depot at Battersea but some, such as fresh milk and bread, had been delivered direct to the platform. Under the watchful eye of the conductor, attendants fitted fresh, clean antimacassars to the head-rest of each seat before laying up the tables.

As the 11.00am departure time approached, attendants stationed themselves at each door to greet passengers, show them to their seats and charge the Pullman supplement to their fare. Once under way, attendants took orders for morning coffee and light refreshments to be served on the one-hour trip, after which the conductor or a leading attendant wrote out bills and collected cash whilst his team cleared the tables. As the train glided to a halt under the curved roof of Brighton station, the attendants once again manned each door to bid a respectful farewell to their customers.

The kitchens may not have been taxed too hard on this first trip but on the return journey, leaving Brighton at 1.25pm, luncheon would be served and each kitchen would be catering for up to 100 passengers. A quick turn-round at Victoria and a service of afternoon tea on the 3.00pm departure was followed by dinners and suppers on the 5.25pm Up, the 7.00pm Down and the 9.15pm Up. At the end of the day the conductor completed his commissary sheet detailing the food, drink and tobacco sold and placed his order for replenishment stock for the next day.

For all its luxury, the Brighton Belle did have an Achilles' heel. In common with other Southern Railway express units of the 1930s, the bogies were of a new design that had originally been developed by the Dutch National Railways. These 'Dutch' bogies, as they were known, were fitted with an equalising beam – a steel bar that connected the front and rear axle-boxes and was attached by springs to the bogie frames. Though the design had presumably worked well enough in Holland, it proved to be unsuited to life on the Southern and the Brighton Belles were notorious rough-riders. R. W. Kidner, a passenger on the inaugural service on 1st January 1933, describes how these rough-riding characteristics asserted themselves from the outset – a group of lady madrigal singers, hired to demonstrate how quiet and smooth the new service was, wobbled disconcertingly as the train got into its stride. In 1933, within a few months of entry into service of the Brighton line express units, the Southern Railway made some modifications to the equalising beam bogies in an attempt to improve the ride but without much effect. British Railways made some further modifications between 1956 and 1958, again with no significant improvement. The ride was lively at any speed above 45mph and wise patrons avoided the soup. In the late 1960s a driver gave the following story:

'Recently I was driving the Belle through Copyhold Junction and the jolt was so bad that I slipped off my seat and was left sprawled on the cab floor, however I managed to keep hold of the controller handle to avoid an emergency brake application. Eventually I regained the *status quo* and finished the journey to Brighton without further incident. As I was closing down the cab, there was a knocking on the cab door window. I espied an elderly lady wishing to talk to me and thought, 'Oh dear – a complaint coming for sure'. Imagine my surprise when she thanked me for a splendid journey and presented me with a box of chocolates. I was speechless!'

Including prototypes (1931), production series (1932) and spares (1933), 109 motor bogies and 216 trailer bogies with equalising beams were assembled. All, or nearly all, remained in use until withdrawal of the 6 PUL units commenced. The bogies were exchanged between units during maintenance and few, if any, which have survived are under their original coaches.

Kitchen of Pullman car 'Doris' pictured at Horsted Keynes in June 2009, showing the cramped conditions under which the chefs had to work. The microwave oven and two-ring hob are, of course, later additions. The pantry was used to prepare beverages and uncooked snacks and also for storage of crockery, cutlery, glassware and other catering equipment. There was additional storage space in cupboards located in the corridor opposite the pantry. Note the oval window incorporating a fresh air ventilator. *Colin Duff*

THE BRIGHTON BELLE

Bill of Fare

SNACK SERVICE

| | | |
|---|---|---|
| Soup of the day with Golden Croutons | | 1/6 |
| Deep Fried Fillet of Fish Tartare with French Fried Potatoes | | 8/6 |
| Pan Fried Egg and Grilled Bacon ( Single ) 4/– | Double | 8/– |
| Welsh Rarebit 2/9 Buck Rarebit | | 4/– |
| Grilled Sirloin Steak with Tomato, French Fried Potatoes and Garden Peas | | 12/6 |
| Sausages (each) 1/2 Bacon (portion) | | 2/9 |
| Tomatoes on Toast | | 2/9 |
| Eggs divers styles (each) | | 1/4 |
| A Pair of Grilled Kippers | | 3/6 |
| Grilled Chipolata Sausages and Whipped Potatoes | | 3/6 |
| Cold Collation and Mixed Dressed Salad | | 8/6 |

BEVERAGES

| | | |
|---|---|---|
| Tea | per pot, per person | 1/6 |
| Coffee | per pot, per person | 2/– |
| Milk | per glass | 1/3 |
| Bovril | per pot, per person | 1/8 |

SANDWICHES (full round)

| | |
|---|---|
| Assorted Centres ( Plain ) | 2/6 |
| Toasted Bacon Sandwich with pickles | 4/– |
| Double Decker Egg and Bacon Sandwich | 5/6 |

SUNDRIES

| | | |
|---|---|---|
| Cut Hovis and White Bread and Butter (two rounds) | | 8d. |
| Buttered Toast (per round) | | 9d. |
| Roll and Curled Butter | | 9d |
| Cheeses : ( Portion ) English Farmhouse 1/3 | Continental | 1/6 |
| Quality Cake | | 9d. |
| Biscuits Sweet (Packet) | | 6d. |
| Biscuits Cheese Dry | | 3d. |
| Individual Preserves, Jam, Honey, Marmalade | | 6d. |

PLEASE ASK FOR A BILL AND RETAIN IT

In case of difficulty will passengers please see the *Conductor*
or write to
*General Manager, British Rail Catering,
14 Bishop's Bridge Road, London, W.2*
enclosing your bill.

# Chapter 12
# Special Duties

Brighton Belle units were occasionally used for royal trains and for VIP specials anywhere on the Southern's third rail electrified network, though a steam or electric locomotive and hauled Pullman cars were also used for some of these workings as these trains could be marshalled more flexibly to meet the specific requirements of the occasion.

The working of royal trains required – and still requires today – considerable detailed planning and confidential instructions to all concerned with their operation. The Pullman company were, of course, deeply involved whenever Pullman cars were used for such services, removing some seats and tables to provide ample room for the royal party, preparing the cars to the highest standards of cleanliness and polish and providing thoughtful extra touches such as bowls of flowers. An appropriate menu would be planned and a Pullman management representative would travel with the train to ensure that the team delivered the on-board service without a hitch.

Unit 3053 conveyed Queen Elizabeth (the Queen Consort) from London to Brighton on 26th March 1948. The unit was attached to the rear of a 6 PUL unit on the 2.00pm from Victoria and returned as part of a 10 BEL formation on the 5.25pm from Brighton.

The Coronation on 2nd June 1953 generated large volumes of special and VIP traffic, with the Pullman car company heavily involved. A party of 300 guests was conveyed from the Metropole Hotel at Brighton on an early (5.05am) 10-car special to Victoria to watch the ceremonial processions, returning from Victoria to Brighton at 7.05pm. This produced the unusual sight of all three Belle units at Victoria at the same time – the third unit had run empty from Streatham Hill to work the regular 7.00pm service to Brighton.

Unit 3052 operated three royal specials in connection with the Coronation Review of the Fleet at Spithead on 15th June 1953. Several members of the Royal Family, including Queen Elizabeth the Queen Mother and Princess Margaret, travelled from Waterloo to Portsmouth Harbour, departing at 12.50pm and arriving at 2.35pm. The Royal party travelled in 'Audrey' and were served luncheon *en route*. The Queen Mother returned to Windsor that evening in unit 3052, leaving Portsmouth Harbour at 6.30pm and arriving at Windsor and Eton Riverside at 8.05pm. The unit promptly returned to Fratton depot (8.35pm–10.20pm) to be prepared for a 9.35am

departure the following day to bring the Queen and the Duke of Edinburgh to Windsor, returning empty to home territory at Streatham Hill.

The following year on 14th April 1954, 3052 was again chosen for a royal journey from Waterloo to Portsmouth & Southsea, conveying the young Prince Charles and Princess Anne to board the newly-commissioned Royal Yacht 'Britannia' for a voyage to Tobruk to be reunited with their parents who were returning from a three-month Royal tour of Australia. According to Julian Morel, Prince Charles was surprised by the absence of a locomotive and enquired whether there was a man at the front. During the journey he and Princess Anne were taken through the train to meet the motorman.

On 13th November 1964 unit 3052 was again the choice for a Royal train from Victoria to Brighton where the Queen visited the campus of the University of Sussex and officially opened the newly completed Library building.

Royalty were not the only users of 'Brighton Belle' units for special trips. One notable occasion was the Machine Tool Trades Association's charter of a 10-car Belle formation to take a party of 300 from Victoria to Hove for a gala ball at Brighton's Royal Pavilion on 3rd July 1956. Guests were served a five-course dinner on the outward journey (departing at 8.42pm and arriving at 9.57pm) and a full English breakfast on the return (1.45am–3.05am). Julian Morel recalls that the promoter of the trip, Major Cyril Dennis, had covered every detail, devising the menus, choosing the wines and selecting the programme of music to be played by the Southern Railway Band as passengers boarded the train at Victoria. He even organised a first-aid post, staffed by a doctor and two nurses, in one of the First Class coupés.

Other occasional special workings used Brighton Belle stock. Unilever chartered a unit for a trip from Blackfriars to Eastbourne on 29th November 1956 and again on 19th April 1961 using unit 3051, whilst unit 3053 was used for a special for AEI from Victoria to Dover Marine on 25th May 1961. Entrepreneur Lionel Burleigh set up a series charter of 5 BEL units each Saturday and Sunday night from 28th and 29th March 1964 onwards. The 'Regency Belle' left Victoria at 19.17 (by now the railway was using the 24-hour clock) and arrived at Brighton at 20.25, with the return journey scheduled to depart at 02.15 and arrive at 03.30.

The publicity for the venture enthused: 'Pass under the gay awning, along the red carpet to the 'Regency Belle', the most luxurious train in the world staffed by efficient stewards and six of Britain's most beautiful girls in immaculate Regency costume, who will escort you to your reserved seat in an atmosphere of soft lighting and very quiet Gershwin music. There will be an orchid for every lady, and on the journey down you sip your vintage champagne and relax …

Upon arrival you will be given a 'V.I.P.' welcome by one of Brighton's celebrated personalities, of whom there are many. A fleet of luxurious cars will then drive you to a first-class hotel where you will partake of a recherché supper in delightful surroundings. After this, dancing; a midnight swim? or a mild flutter at the gaming tables and then – idle chatter until your carriage arrives at 1.45 to transport you back to your softly heated luxury train.

Then the perfect English breakfast will be served as only this Country knows how to cook it. Finian Haddock, crisp Wiltshire bacon, Sussex eggs, buttered toast and chunky marmalade with tea or coffee. All this and the morning papers too!

A night to remember and the cost £7 7s 0d.'

However, the idea did not catch on. The Sunday run lasted only a couple of weekends and the Saturday run was cancelled from April 25th due to lack of support.

## AFTERNOON TEA

4/6

A Variety of Assorted Sandwiches

Toasted Tea Cake

Hovis and White Bread and Butter

Preserves

Fruit Cake          Plain Cake

Assorted Pastries          Biscuits

Pot of Tea
(Indian or China)

PLEASE ASK FOR A BILL AND RETAIN IT

In case of difficulty please see the Conductor or write to General Manager British Rail Catering 14, Bishop's Bridge Road, London, W.2

Unit 3053 heads south on the Quarry Line on a summer's day as its customers sample the delights of the menu. This rural spot looks very different today, with the eight-lane M25 motorway passing under the railway. *Colour-Rail*

# Chapter 13
# A Trip to London – 1967

Let us take another trip on the Belle. We spent rather a long time in Brighton after our previous journey as it is now an autumn morning in 1967. Much has changed in the intervening 31 years. The former Southern Railway is now the Southern Region of British Railways and the Pullman Car Co. is no longer independent although our now elderly 5 BEL units are still resplendent in their traditional umber and cream Pullman livery, the only change being a bright yellow warning panel under the windows on the cab fronts.

The rush hour has passed as we again make our way to platform 6 for the 09.40 departure to London. The commuters have all left earlier and the trains arriving convey only a few shoppers and students heading towards Sussex University and Brighton Polytechnic.

Brighton station, although much the same under its curving roof, has lost its services to Horsham and to the Dyke, while the train to Uckfield, now operated by a diesel-electric multiple unit, will shortly be history as well. The real change is in the rolling stock. The Belle's original express sisters, the 6 PUL and 6 PAN units, have all gone – scrapped, or temporarily reformed into a few 6 COR units to serve out their last days on specials and relief trains before they join their siblings at the scrapyard. A few of the distinctive pre-war 4 LAV, 2 BIL and 2 HAL units remain, although these have mostly been relegated to secondary duties along the Coastway route.

The express services are now operated by new 4-car units to British Railways' standard design, coded 4 CIG and 4 BIG units. Why Cig and Big? As with the pre-war 4 COR and 4 BUF units 'C' stood for 'Corridor' and 'B' for Buffet whilst IG was the old LBSCR telegraphic code for Brighton. The semifast and slow services are being taken over by the ubiquitous 4 VEP units (Vestibule Electro-Pneumatic, meaning that they had corridors and the standard electrically actuated pneumatic brake) which made their debut on Bournemouth line services the previous year. These are something of a design compromise, with high density 5-abreast seating compared with the pre-war units' deep cushioned comfort but with a through corridor and lavatory access for all. Back on the Belle, as a special treat, we settle into the deep, cushioned seats of a still luxurious, if a little faded, First Class carriage to take breakfast. Bells ring, whistles are blown, green flags waved and, almost imperceptibly, the Belle slips away from the seaside.

1966 was the last full year in which both the Brighton and Bournemouth Belles operated. The latter was withdrawn, along with the last mainline steam services in the UK, on July 9th 1967, leaving just the Golden Arrow and Brighton Belle to continue the Pullman tradition on Southern metals. The artist who designed this brochure was clearly a stickler for accuracy, though 'Mona' (from 5 BEL unit 3053) actually had more equipment below the solebar than depicted in the advertisement. *Anthony Ford Collection*

One of the new 4 VEP units, which replaced the 4 LAVs, enters Brighton station in the summer of 1967 as the Belle prepares to depart for London. The signal box that was built in 1932 to operate newly installed colour-light signalling as part of the Brighton line electrification project is still there on the right but nothing remains of the former Brighton loco works. *John Scrace*

There's no more enjoyable way of travelling quickly between London and Brighton or Bournemouth than by these luxurious all-Pullman trains.

It's just sixty minutes to Brighton and two and a quarter hours to Bournemouth — time well spent in complete relaxation and the enjoyment of excellent food and wine. The number of passengers is strictly

**BRIGHTON OR BOURNEMOUTH IN PULLMAN LUXURY**

limited to the seats available — be sure of yours when the occasion arises. One day — and they run every day of the year except 25th and 26th December — you'll be glad you went by one of the Belles.

By August 1968, the Pullman supplement had risen to 'half a crown' (two shillings and sixpence), and by June 1971 to 20p (four shillings in old money). *Anthony Ford Collection*

A little faded, but still comfortable. Interior of a Second Class trailer in June 1966. *Fred Matthews*

Another view at Brighton. Note the trolley laden with mailbags on the opposite platform with the maroon-liveried parcels van waiting. The 'hot dog' Brighton totem is also visible. Both mail trains and totems are now just memories. *John Scrace*

The Belle heads into Brighton, passing the Pullman works and a carriage washer on the Lovers' Walk head-shunt. BR's new main line livery, the blue-and-grey scheme seen on the locomotive-hauled stock to the right, will soon adorn (or despoil?) the Belle. *Colour Rail*

Brighton motive power depot is on our left but there are now no more steam trains to leave a haze of smoke, just a lone electro-diesel, that unique concept of an electric locomotive with auxiliary diesel power that reminds us of the Southern's penchant for doing things differently. On our right, Brighton Works stands empty. It will soon be demolished to make way for a large car park. Preston Park Pullman Works still stands, but Pullman car maintenance was transferred away in 1963. Now empty, it seems to have an exciting future ahead as a railway transport museum and already contains a few historic steam engines, carriages and wagons.

We head north, through the Brighton suburbs and the tunnels at Patcham and Clayton and the country station of Hassocks. In contrast to our last journey, the goods yard at this and nearly all the other stations *en route* to London are either empty or have been replaced by a car park, full of commuters' cars. Road transport, for both passengers and freight, is now the dominant mode in Britain. Nevertheless, despite the modernising ambitions of the BR Design Panel, most of the stations remain in the characteristic green-and-cream Southern Region livery, with each concrete lamp post adorned with a green totem proclaiming the station's identity.

The Belle heads south through Hassocks. This country station has an extensive goods yard, once used for marshalling wagons for the 'East Coastway' (Brighton-Littlehampton) route and Brighton. Now the closest station to the South Downs, since closure of the Devil's Dyke branch, it is a popular destination for ramblers and is the railhead for the charming village of Ditchling. *Colour Rail*

## "BRIGHTON BELLE"

### BREAKFAST SERVICE

Cereals : Cornflakes 1/-   Special "K" 1/-   Frosties 1/—
Fruit Juices : Pineapple 1/6   Tomato 1/6   Orange 1/6

Eggs Styled to Choice (each) 1/4
Grilled Bacon (portion) 2/9
Grilled Frankfurter or Cambridge Sausage (each) 1/2
Grilled Kippers (Single) 1/9   (Pair) 3/6
Hot Buttered Toast (Per Round) 9d.
Dry Toast & Curled Butter (Single) 10d.   (Double) 1/8
Individual Preserves 6d.

Tea per pot 1/6

Coffee per pot 2/—

### PLEASE ASK FOR A BILL AND RETAIN IT

In case of difficulty will passengers please see the Conductor
or write to
General Manager, British Rail Catering, 14, Bishop's Bridge Road, London, W.2
enclosing your bill.

We peruse the breakfast menu. Shall we have kippers? We flash through Haywards Heath, bouncing wildly. A glimpse to the right reveals a branch line diverging away from us through the trees. This was once an electrified line to Horsted Keynes but now only runs to a goods depot at Ardingly. For a few years from 1959, the branch was used first to store newly-built electric multiple units for the Kent Coast electrification scheme and then withdrawn loco-hauled coaches, but these have all departed now. We shall meet the electrics again later. Between 1960 and 1963, the line provided access to the fledgling Bluebell Line railway which started operations from Sheffield Park with a Stroudley 'Terrier' tank engine and two redundant coaches bought from British Railways for £750. As one of the pioneers of the heritage railway movement, the Bluebell was able to acquire an enviable collection of steam locos and rolling stock and is now one of the World's premier preserved railways.

The Ouse Valley viaduct is as magical as ever, but we are distracted by the arrival of coffee and the smell of frying bacon and eggs approaching Balcombe. The train is busy today and we hope we will have time for our meal but as we pass the still busy yards at Three Bridges, a silver platter arrives at our shoulder and breakfast is served.

The 1966 breakfast menu, with the infamous kippers!
*Anthony Ford collection*

Haywards Heath. This is a major commuter railhead serving not only the town itself but the suburbs of Lindfield and Cuckfield and a string of villages along the A272, from Cowfold in the west to Newick and Chailey in the east. Even when the Bluebell line was open, it was always quicker to drive to Haywards Heath and take one of the frequent electric trains arriving in London about 45 minutes later. The goods yard was soon replaced by a large car park to serve this traffic. Note that the Belle only has 9 cars. One vehicle must have been away for repair during the time this photo was taken on Sunday 27th August 1967. *John Scrace*

The magnificent Ouse Valley viaduct, which traverses a very small stream, part of the nascent River Ouse which exits to the sea at Newhaven. Remarkably, barges were taken along the Ouse to this point conveying the bricks for the viaduct's construction. *John Scrace*

The 15.00 Victoria-Brighton Belle service headed by unit 3051 approaches Balcombe station on the 31st May 1968. *John Scrace*

The area north of the Ouse Valley viaduct and south of Three Bridges is blessed with the extensive Ashdown Forest and is probably the most beautiful location on the Belle's route, particularly in spring when the woodlands are carpeted in Bluebells. The Forest abounds with roe and fallow deer, which are often glimpsed at the railside in early morning and evening. A band of red sandstone traverses the Forest and is pierced by Balcombe Tunnel, from which the Belle is seen emerging. Shortly after leaving the tunnel, the line divides into Up and Down Fast and Up and Down Slow lines (four tracks) and remains so all the way to Victoria. *John Scrace*

At platform 6, another diesel-electric multiple unit waits with a service to East Grinstead but, like most of the other Wealden lines, this will succumb to Dr Beeching's axe on New Year's eve. Three Bridges, though, is no longer a country junction surrounded by fields but now part of the rapidly-expanding Crawley New Town, one of the post-war developments that ring London, providing clean new homes, schools and jobs for those relocating from the city. One of the authors was raised in Crawley, but the umbilical link with his family was never broken, and nearly every weekend he was returned to the family roots in the Beckenham/Bromley area usually in father's car rather than a BIL or HAL unit from Ifield to East Croydon and the No. 54 bus.

We are now on the racing ground and, following the major recast of the Southern Region timetable in July 1967, all Victoria-Brighton non-stop services have to do the run in 55 minutes.

Approaching Gatwick, there are major changes. Although the platforms of the 1936 Gatwick Airport station still stand, the footbridge and all buildings have been demolished. The 'Beehive' terminal is still there, but no longer serves air passengers and is overshadowed by a large hangar outside of which sits a variety of helicopters – a mode of transport in

Opposite: A whole chapter could be written about the impact of Gatwick Airport on Brighton line services, but, suffice to say, the Belle never called there even for a special working. This 1963 picture shows the complex track-work, one line proceeding from the Up Fast, across both Slow lines and directly to the electrified carriage sidings. Such complexity is both expensive to maintain and would produce a considerable jolt to passing trains. The layout in 2011 is much simplified, with an additional Up Slow running line from Tinsley Green to Gatwick Airport station, and only three electrified carriage sidings. In the 1960s, they were used to stable a variety of 2 BIL, 2 HAL and (from the summer of 1967) 4 VEP units, that were used to strengthen services from the Sussex coast (mostly the slow Bognor Regis and Horsham services) to accommodate passengers to and from the airport. At the time, there were few scheduled flights from Gatwick and most extra capacity was needed for the numerous charter flights that left for the Spanish Costas and other European destinations as the package holiday boom grew. From 1968, Gatwick had a service every 15 minutes from Victoria with a dedicated hourly non-stop during the summer operated by a 4 VEP. *Colour Rail*

Below: The Belle heads south through Three Bridges. Many happy hours were spent train-spotting here by one of the authors. The line is dead straight and expresses pass at maximum speed. The passage of the Belle was always the most impressive! *John Scrace*

its infancy 30 years ago. A roar makes us look upwards as a BAC 1-11 jetliner of British United Airways passes overhead to touch down on Gatwick Airport's lengthened 7000ft runway. We get a quick glimpse of more planes at Gatwick, BAC 1-11s and VC-10s in the colours of British United Airways, de Havilland Comets owned by Dan-Air and a variety of turboprop aircraft, Bristol Britannias, Handley-Page Heralds, and Vickers Viscounts, before passing through the 'new'

Gatwick Airport station opened in 1958 on the site of the former Racecourse station and integrated into the new terminal of what is now London's second airport. To accommodate the increasing number of passengers using the airport, many of the services to and from the Mid-Sussex line attach and detach one of the slightly more modern Bulleid 'tin' 2 HAL units here, although a dedicated Gatwick Airport-Victoria service using the brand new 4 VEP units was introduced in July.

This picture, taken in July 1967, gives a better view of the unelectrified sidings adjacent to the Down Fast. These were often used to stable condemned wagons and electric multiple units. One of the authors remembers two of the short-lived 6 COR units spending months here from late 1968 until their final journey to the scrapyard. Next to the sidings is a very interesting feature. What appears to be a single telegraph wire is, in fact, an early warning system. Should a plane crash on the approach to the runway and break this wire, all the signals will turn to red and an alert will sound in the nearby Three Bridges signalling control centre. There have been a few 'false alarms' when large birds struck the wire, but only one crash has occurred at Gatwick Airport to date and that was several miles distant. The fields are now covered by the airport's extensive car parks and a plane passes overhead every few minutes. It is worth commenting on the planes that could be seen in 1967. The turboprop aircraft visible to the left of the runway is outside the British United Airways hangar, and is almost certainly a Bristol 175 Britannia. Around 1965, BUA withdrew its Britannias from passenger service and replaced them with BAC 1-11 and VC-10 jets, so this example is likely to be a freighter employed on BUA's Africargo service. At the time, BUA and Dan-Air were the only airlines using Gatwick for year-round scheduled services. The contrast with today is unimaginable! *John Scrace*

The Belle is flying along now, roaring through Horley, Salfords, Earlswood, along the Quarry line and into Coulsdon where the buses on the A23 below us magically change from green to red. We plunge into a roofless tunnel – the former covered way at Cane Hill was uncovered in 1955 – and head towards Croydon. The town is virtually unrecognisable from the market town it was 30 years ago. All around us, skyscrapers are rising into the sky, transforming Croydon into a major commercial, business and residential area. East Croydon station, however, remains reassuringly dingy but is desperately in need of modernisation to deal with its huge commuter traffic.

After sweeping through East Croydon, we part company with the London Bridge route at Windmill Bridge Junction and bear left towards Victoria. The Norwood marshalling yards and Selhurst electric multiple unit (EMU) depot are to our left and as we pass through Selhurst station, we note that the Selhurst Park ground of Crystal Palace football club has now gained large floodlights on pylons. 'The Glaziers' are doing well in the Second Division, and may be in the First Division soon! However, on the higher ground around Crystal Palace, two even taller structures catch our eye. First, at 499ft high is the Croydon transmitter, and a little further to the east is the Crystal Palace transmitter which, at 719ft high, is the tallest structure in Britain. These beam television pictures all over the greater London area, the older Crystal Palace transmitter sending programmes from the BBC, while the Croydon one transmits those from ITV.

Now, less than 15 minutes from London, we finish our breakfast and coffee as the suburbs of South London pass by the windows. In the air, a procession of jetliners from such famous companies as BOAC, BEA, PanAm and TWA head towards Heathrow. On entering Clapham Junction, we are, sadly, no longer distracted by Oliver Bulleid's streamlined Pacifics or Robert Riddles' robust Standard steam engines hauling long lines of green carriages towards Dorset and the West Country. The last bastion of main line steam, the Bournemouth line, succumbed to electrification this July and one can now reach Bournemouth in as little as 100 minutes, pushed by a 4 REP EMU developing 3200 hp, nearly twice that of our 5 BEL unit. The line to Exeter has fared even worse. Nearly all the ex-Southern lines west of Salisbury have been ripped up and the route of the 'Atlantic Coast Express' now has only one diesel-hauled semi-fast train every two hours.

Our bill is paid as we swing over the LSWR line to Waterloo, past the smoky towers of the monolithic Battersea power station, now with four smoking chimneys since Battersea 'B' came on line in 1953, and glide down Grosvenor Bank towards our destination. Main line services to Kent and the Channel Ports of Dover and Folkestone from the 'Chatham side' of Victoria, are now in the hands of the 4 CEP and 4 BEP EMUs that were once temporarily stored on the Haywards Heath-Horsted Keynes line. However the 'Golden Arrow' Pullman service from Victoria to Dover Marine, which will leave at 11:00, is now in the capable hands of a powerful 'E5000' (later Class 71) electric locomotive.

There is a complex of junctions and stations around Streatham. The Belle is heading south towards Streatham Common station while the line to London Bridge via Streatham, Tulse Hill and Peckham Rye heads off to the right. The Southern Railway 'Odeon' style signalbox controls the flying junctions from the Wimbledon/Mitcham Junction–Streatham lines on to the fast and slow Brighton lines. At this time, these were traversed by mainline services via the Mid-Sussex line from Portsmouth, Bognor Regis and Horsham to Victoria. Nowadays, these trains have been diverted to serve Crawley and Gatwick Airport and, arguably, the towns of Dorking and Sutton are less well-served than previously.
*John Scrace*

One of the most-photographed railway locations in London is where the Brighton line passes through Wandsworth Common. The line is flanked on both sides by footpaths and Catsback Bridge crosses the line in the background. A Belle heads south. *John Scrace*

And what are those blue, French-looking carriages with their gold legend *'Compagnie Internationale des Wagons Lits et des Grands Express Européens'* that we see entering Grosvenor Road carriage sheds for servicing? Ah, *mon ami*, that is the rolling stock of the 'Night Ferry' service that arrived from Paris and Brussels an hour or so before us, the carriages and vans having been loaded on to a train ferry for the crossing from Dunkirk to Dover. They will return to the Continent tonight and be in Paris and Brussels by 09.00 tomorrow. The romance of the railways was in the air on that morning.

Our journey is over, but the Belle will be heading back to Sussex at 11.00, so the staff are already preparing her for another load of passengers. Shafts of light filter through the cracked glass panes in the high, vaulted roof of the Brighton side of Victoria, still stained with soot and encrusted with pigeon droppings, as we make our way towards the rather less glamorous red or silver trains of the District Line from the Underground station, which has just become much busier with the recent opening of the new Victoria Line to Oxford Circus, Euston and King's Cross.

First Class car 'Audrey' awaits custom. The light footbridge deserves explanation. In May 1962, London's first rail-air terminal was opened at Victoria for British United Airways. This steel and glass building was 15ft above the cab road at the far end of platforms 15-17 and outgoing passengers used the footbridge to reach platforms 11-17 from the terminal. In 1965, 230,000 BUA passengers used the facility. *John Scrace*

# Chapter 14
# The Blue Belle

The Pullman Car Company had been acquired by the State-owned British Transport Commission (BTC) in 1954 and ownership of the Pullman business had passed to the British Railways Board when the BTC was abolished in 1962. Pullman ceased to be a separate entity within BR when the Hotels and Catering Executive was abolished in 1967, after which the 'Brighton Belle' came under the direct control of the Southern Region of British Railways. By now, the Belle's 1930s-vintage sister fleets had been replaced on the Brighton line by the new CIG/BIG fleet of express electric multiple units. In the 'Swinging Sixties', and alongside the new fleet, the three 5 BEL units in their traditional Pullman livery looked thoroughly out of date.

However, the 5 BEL units were by no means life-expired. Only one or two of the three units was normally in traffic at any one time and the fleet had been stored for much of the war so cumulative unit mileages were relatively low. The sturdy all-steel cars had been well maintained and did not have serious corrosion problems. The Belle's regular clientele included a considerable number of celebrities such as the actors Dora Bryan, Alan Melville, Dame Flora Robson and Lord Olivier who lived in Brighton and commuted regularly to London and they lobbied hard for the service to be retained. In 1968 British Railways decided to give the three units an overhaul and facelift. The work was carried out at BR's re-fitted former locomotive works at Eastleigh because the Pullman workshops at Preston Park had been closed by BR in 1963.

The Southern Region dropped the Pullman brand name and replaced the traditional umber and cream external livery with BR's new blue and light grey corporate house-style. In place of the former car names or abbreviated numbers, the words 'Brighton Belle' were displayed centrally on the lower bodysides of each car, with BR's double-arrow logo towards the outer ends of the motor coaches and each car's full 3-digit schedule number towards the inner ends. Internally, the seats were re-upholstered in Inter-City 70 moquette – charcoal and grey (First Class) or blue and green check (Second Class), with mustard carpets, orange curtains and green sun blinds. Mercifully, the refurbishers left the original interior panelling and fittings largely intact, facilitating later restoration.

Unit 3052 was the first to be outshopped and made its first run in blue and grey livery on 23rd December 1968 on the

The charcoal and grey upholstery used in the First Class vehicles was identical to that adorning the First Class seating of the newly-introduced REP/TC stock on the Bournemouth line. The mustard carpets and orange curtains are also visible in this view of 'Doris' (or should we say, Car 282) at Horsted Keynes after preservation. Thankfully, the marquetry and other finishings were left untouched. *Colin Duff*

In contrast, the Second Class vehicles looked far worse. The common-or-garden blue-and-green check moquette and bright orange curtains may have looked fine on a 4 VEP, but did nothing for the art deco splendour of the Belle. Most of the marquetry remained. *Fred Matthews*

Tray produced to mark the end of the Belle. The text on the tray read: 'Today is the end of an era. The final chapter in an unforgettable episode in railway history. The last run of the Brighton Belle. It's goodbye to Hazel, Doris, Audrey, Vera, Gwen and Mona and their frilly lamp shades and old world charm. It's a sad day. We will miss them. But one can't survive on nostalgia. Let us remember them fondly but realistically – as ladies in retirement. What of tomorrow? Vast modernisation schemes are already being implemented. New stations are replacing the old. Faster trains are bringing centres closer together. And plans are well advanced to improve facilities not only on trains but stations, and to spread the service until it covers not merely the best in food and drinks, but whatever travellers may need. It's a lot to do, and in the doing of it some once popular services will go the way of the Brighton Belle. Sad – but there it is. We must utilise our resources where they are most needed – to invest in a service for today's traveller. Our intentions are clear. Our aims and ambitions are to give you, the traveller, the finest, most up-to-date service you've ever known.'

09.25 from Brighton, coupled to another unit in the original colours. The other two units were then similarly overhauled; 3051 was completed in February 1969 and 3053 in May of that year. Each of these acquired roller-blind headcode panels in place of the original stencil arrangement and 3052 was similarly modified the following year. All three units were fitted with COR motors and gears which had been held as spares.

On 12th September 1969 Kitchen First 279 of unit 3051 suffered an electrical fire whilst waiting in Brighton station to form the 09.40 service to Victoria. Much of the damage was done by the Brighton Fire Brigade who used axes to hack away marquetry and ceiling panels to access the smouldering wiring. The unit returned to traffic in January 1970 temporarily with four cars until repairs were completed on the fifth.

By now, illuminated red squares in the roller blinds in the headcode panel of the rear coach of BEL units had replaced the time-honoured oil lamp to indicate the rear of the train, as seen here on one leaving Brighton. *John Scrace*

In addition to their quotidian duties, 'Brighton Belle' units continued to operate occasional specials. These included a trip from Charing Cross to Brighton on 15th November 1969, from Victoria to Borough Green on 18th July 1970 and from Victoria to Glynde (back from Lewes) on 14th August 1970 for Glyndebourne Opera passengers. 1970 is famous in the annals of railway history as the date of the Battle of the Kippers. One morning, the renowned actor Lord Olivier was looking forward to his usual breakfast kippers as he boarded the 09.25 Belle service at Brighton, only to be told that they were no longer available due to 'economies'. In the manner of Henry the Fifth rallying his troops at Agincourt, Lord Olivier whipped up support among influential Belle regulars for his campaign to have kippers reinstated. The battle was brief and victory decisive, with BR quickly restoring them to the 'Belle' breakfast menu.

However, the reality was that customer support for the Brighton Belle was ebbing away. BR's need for economies was genuine as fewer and fewer people were taking meals on the train, making it harder to justify the large team of on-board staff. As we noted in our 1967 trip, the journey time of all non-stop services from Victoria to Brighton had been reduced from 60 to 55 minutes and whilst this was well within the power capabilities of the elderly units it did accentuate their rough riding problems, especially as passengers were now comparing them to the new standard fleet. The modern livery only made the units look even more out of date and interiors that we now appreciate as art deco gems then simply looked old fashioned and dowdy. In short, customers increasingly resented paying a premium for an inferior ride on an ageing train with an on-board service that they did not want.

By 1972 the UK economy was in trouble and rail passenger numbers in sharp decline. With the Belle units due for another overhaul, withdrawal was inevitable. The last 'Brighton Belle' services ran on Sunday 30th April 1972, the day before the Southern Region's new summer timetable came into force.

Summer at Balcombe, as a London-bound Belle is seen through the over-bridge at the country end of the station. Passengers can board 12-car trains at the end of the down platform, but are not advised to enter this very narrow region when expresses are passing! *John Scrace*

The Belle heads down the Quarry line towards Brighton. Although this area looks very rural, the train will shortly pass the British Industrial Sand works at Holmethorpe on its left and a sea of light industrial units on its right. By 2011, the BIS works had been swept away and replaced by housing. *John Scrace*

A quiet interlude at platform 16 at Victoria in 1970 as the water tanks are filled. Note the plates hung over the doors to indicate the car numbers for those with reserved seats. *Michael Baker*

Supplementary fares of 20 or 30p to travel in luxury. *Colin Duff from the museum on Platforms 1 and 2, Horsted Keynes, Bluebell Railway*

In the autumn of her life, the Belle heads for Brighton near Hassocks. *Michael Baker*

# Chapter 15
# Belle Performance

All railway operations run to a strict timetable to ensure that the capacity of a particular route (in this case, London Victoria to Brighton) is optimised for both passenger and freight trains and that the time taken between two points is commercially viable. The famous slogan 'Every hour, on the hour, in the hour' marketed by the Southern Railway to describe its non-stop Victoria-Brighton electric service in 1933 would not have been possible if both the trains and the track layout were not designed for this purpose.

The fleet of express trains used on this route, the 6 PUL, 6 PAN, 6 CIT and 5 BEL units, were mechanically and electrically similar and were sufficiently powerful to achieve the 60-minute schedule with relative ease. Time for some physics. One relevant factor here is the 'Power to Weight ratio' (p:w), which is obtained by dividing the available power (in this case,

horsepower) by the trains' weight in tons. So, a 10-car unladen BEL rake will weigh 498 tons and, with 3,600hp available will give a p:w ratio of 7.2 hp per ton. The equivalent 12-car PUL/PAN rake weighs in at 266+244 = 510 tons, with the same 3,600hp, giving a p:w ratio of 7.1. In contrast, a 12-car CIG/BIG/CIG rake is both lighter and has less power, the weight being 151+154.5+151 = 456.5 tons and with 3,000hp available, the p:w ratio drops to 6.6. On this basis, we'd expect the BEL and PUL/PAN rakes to behave pretty similarly, while the CIG/BIG stock would be a little slower off the starting blocks.

But it's not quite as simple as that. As a train accelerates, the power plant (in this case, the traction motors), has to get the unit to the desired speed by overcoming the inertia of the train, the friction ('rolling resistance') of the wheel and motor bearings and drag on the train body as it moves through air. A

Speed restricted location: 50mph – Earlswood (Sand) Tunnel. *John Scrace*

further factor is the design of the traction electrical equipment and the ratios of the gears through which the motors drive the axles, which represent a trade-off between power on the one hand and starting tractive effort on the other. The CIG/BIG stock had a smoother body profile and roller bearings that significantly lowered their rolling resistance compared to the BEL units and actually gave a better performance with less power consumption. However, both classes of unit show less than sparkling performance at speeds above 70mph and anything at 75mph or over tends to be gravity assisted – i.e., downhill.

The performance of a particular locomotive or multiple unit is only one factor that contributes to a service running to time. Others include the geography of the route – uphill and downhill gradients, the radius of curves and the proportion of curved to straight track – maximum speed limits, which are driven by factors such as signal sighting distances, the condition of the track and by the geometry of trackwork through stations and junctions, headways – the minimum distance between one train and another on the same line, which depend on the length and number of block sections – and the power available – 660V at the substation but dropping to the mid 500s or less in the third rail depending on distance from the supply point and the current drawn by other trains in the vicinity; a nominal 600V was assumed.

Before we consider how 'fit for purpose' the 5 BEL units were, and how they compare to their sisters (the PUL/PAN/CIT fleet) and 'grandchildren' (the replacement CIG/BIG stock), it is necessary to look at the Victoria-Brighton route in more detail.

Topographically, the route presented its builders with a number of engineering problems, in particular, the crossing of the chalk North and South Downs and the High Weald sandstone ridge between Three Bridges and Haywards Heath. Like most lines built in the earlier part of the nineteenth century, gradients were fairly modest to enable the relatively underpowered steam locomotives of the 1840s and 1850s to cope. The Downs and the High Weald were dealt with by the boring of substantial tunnels – Quarry for the North Downs, Balcombe for the High Weald and Clayton for the South Downs, with smaller tunnels at Redhill, Haywards Heath and Patcham. In addition, the valley carved by the infant River Ouse is crossed by Mocatta's magnificent Ouse Valley viaduct, trains have to heave themselves up Grosvenor Bank on departing Victoria to cross the Thames and even Brighton station itself is perched high up on a chalk hill. The result of all this is that the line is a switchback, mostly up-and-down at 1 in 264 (i.e., the line climbs or falls 1 yard for every 264 yards travelled), between East Croydon and Brighton. So, it's up for 8 miles to clear the North Downs at Quarry Tunnel, down for 7 miles to Horley, up for 6½ miles to Balcombe Tunnel then

down for 7 miles to Keymer Junction. Finally, up for 5½ miles to pierce the South Downs at the south end of Clayton Tunnel and then a last 5 miles downhill into Brighton.

Next, the track layouts must be considered. The Brighton line has always been extremely busy and, to cope with the ever-increasing traffic, the line was quadrupled between London and the north entrance of Balcombe Tunnel between 1894 and 1910. The line becomes double track from here to traverse the tunnel and the Ouse Valley, then briefly reverts to four tracks from Copyhold Junction and through Haywards Heath station. The rest of the line is double track, until the Brighton suburbs are reached at Preston Park where four lines become available to enter the Brighton terminus.

Upon electrification, a speed limit of 60mph applied in the London suburbs, reducing to 45mph for the junctions at Balham and 40mph through East Croydon. Once clear of Croydon, 75mph was allowed up to 1967, when the speed increased to 80 although trains still had to slow to 50mph at the divergence and convergence of the Quarry Line at Coulsdon North and Earlswood near Redhill.

A quick bit of simple arithmetic would indicate that, at these speeds, the 50-mile run could be achieved in 50 minutes as the LBSCR originally proposed, but the sheer volume of traffic precluded a faster schedule until major engineering and resignalling work in the 1980s raised the line speed to 90mph from South Croydon to Brighton. This eased the Coulsdon and Earlswood restrictions and the journey time between Victoria and Brighton was shortened from 60 to 55 minutes.

The Brighton expresses therefore had to respect the timetable. There was little point in hurtling from Croydon to Hassocks at 75mph only to be met by a succession of yellow and red signals all the rest of the way to Brighton as one caught up the preceding stopping service. In fact, the only time when hard running was required was if the train had been delayed en route and the motorman had to notch up to reach the coast or city within the hour. With the installed power of the BEL units, this was something of a pushover, and, as the Belle services avoided both morning and evening peaks, seriously late running was a rare event. The highest speeds, if required, would be on the downhill, straight stretches between Earlswood and Balcombe Tunnel Junction, then, provided nothing got in the way at Haywards Heath or Keymer Junction, another whiz to Clayton Tunnel.

Tables 1 and 2 overleaf show typical pre- and post-1967 down runs with the Belle and compare them to their contemporary sisters, the PUL/PAN and CIG/BIG stock on the 60- and 55-minute schedules, respectively. Tables 3 and 4 show performance in the Up direction.

Table 1: Up runs (Brighton-Victoria), comparing BEL and PUL/PAN stock (pre-1967, 60 minute schedule).
(tsr = temporary speed restriction; sigs = signals; sch = schedule; * speed-restricted location)

| Run | | | 1 | | 2 | |
|---|---|---|---|---|---|---|
| Date | | | 2.10.57 | | 10.10.64 | |
| Train | | | 17:25 | | 16:25 | |
| Stock | | | BEL | | PUL | |
| Units | | | 3051/2 | | 3003/3008 | |
| Vehicles/Weight (empty)/Weight (full) | | | 10/498/520 | | 12/532/554 | |
| Recorder | | | R.Howlett | | B.Nathan | |
| Timing point | Miles | Schedule (min) | Min:sec | Speed (mph) | Min:sec | Speed (mph) |
| BRIGHTON | 0 | 0 | - | - | - | - |
| Preston Park | 1.29 | | 2:53 | 58 | 2:29 | 48 |
| Patcham Tunnel North | 2.70 | | - | - | 4:07 | 56 |
| Clayton Tunnel South | 4.70 | | - | - | 6:09 | 60 |
| Hassocks | 7.03 | | 8:47 | 63 | 8:14 | 74 |
| Burgess Hill | 9.03 | | 10:44 | 60 | 9:49 | 78 |
| Wivelsfield | 9.80 | 12 | 11:31 | 60 | 10:27 | 79 |
| Haywards Heath | 12.80 | 15 1/2 | 14:29 | 64 | 12:42 tsr | 72 29 |
| Copyhold Junction | 13.99 | | - | - | 14:00 | 29 |
| Balcombe | 16.71 | | 17:06 | 64 | 17:37 | 59 |
| Balcombe Tunnel Junction | 18.85 | | - | - | 19:42 | 67 |
| Three Bridges | 21.26 | 24 1/2 | 22:19 | 65 | 21:43 | 73 |
| Gatwick Airport | 23.94 | | 24:01 | 65 | 23:58 | 69 |
| Horley | 24.78 | 32 | 28:01 tsr | 61 | 24:43 | 67 |
| Salfords | 27.03 | | - | - | 26:46 | 65 |
| Earlswood | 28.90 | | 32:27 | 61 | 28:42 | 47* |
| Quarry Tunnel South | 32.11 | | - | - | 32:23 | 58 |
| Star Lane | 33.81 | | - | - | 34:05 sigs | 62 |
| Coulsdon North | 35.79 | 39 1/2 | 39:44 | 54 | 36:27 | 36 |
| Purley | 37.25 | | 40:48 | 55 | 38:30 | 46 |
| Purley Oaks | 38.18 | | 41:47 | 56 | - | - |
| South Croydon | 39.36 | | 43:02 | 55 | 41:15 | 46 |
| East Croydon | 40.24 | 44 | 45:14 sigs | 15 | 42:39 | 32* |
| Selhurst | 41.43 | | 48:14 | 55 | 44:18 | 52 |
| Thornton Heath | 42.15 | | 50:03 | 56 | - | - |
| Norbury | 43.35 | | 50:23 | 56 | 46:12 | 62 |
| Streatham Common | 44.21 | 49 1/2 | 51:17 | 56 | 47:04 | 58 |
| Balham | 46.15 | | - | - | 49:16 | 49 |
| Wandsworth Common | 46.74 | | - | - | 49:58 sigs | 51 16 |
| Clapham Junction | 48.11 | 51 1/2 | 56:42 | 46 | 52:52 | - |
| Battersea Park | 49.59 | | - | - | 56:25 | - |
| VICTORIA | 50.71 | 59 | 62:19 | - | 59:13 | - |

Table 2: Down runs (Victoria-Brighton), comparing BEL, PUL/PAN and CIG/BIG stock (pre-1967, 60-minute schedule) (tsr = temporary speed restriction; sigs = signals; sch = schedule; * speed-restricted location)

| Run | | | 3 | | 4 | | 5 | |
|---|---|---|---|---|---|---|---|---|
| Date | | | 16.8.64 | | 10.10.64 | | 29.1.66 | |
| Train | | | 08:00 | | 15:00 | | 09:00 | |
| Stock | | | PUL/PAN | | BEL | | CIG/BIG | |
| Units | | | 3015/3026 | | 3052/3 | | 7038/7320 | |
| Vehicles/Weight (empty)/Weight (full) | | | 12/510/532 | | 10/498/520 | | 8/306/330 | |
| Recorder | | | C.Foss | | B.Nathan | | M.Barrett | |
| Timing point | Miles | Schedule (min) | Min:sec | Speed (mph) | Min:sec | Speed (mph) | Min:sec | Speed (mph) |
| VICTORIA | 0.00 | 0 | 0:00 | - | 0:00 | - | 0:00 | - |
| Battersea Park | 1.13 | | 3:15 | - | 3:17 | - | 3:02 | 43/39* |
| Clapham Junction | 2.60 | 7 1/2 | 5:10 | 53 | 5:30 | 51 | 5:08 | 44 |
| Wandsworth Common | 3.98 | | 6:41 | 53 | 7:03 | 54 | 6:58 | 53 |
| Balham | 4.56 | | 7:20 | 47* | 7:44 | 48* | 7:40 | 45* |
| Streatham Common | 6.50 | [3] | 9:30 | 64 | 9:56 | 60 | 9:56 | 56 |
| Norbury | 7.36 | | 10:18 | 64 | 10:46 (sigs) | 63 | 10:45 (sigs) | 55/58 |
| Selhurst | 9.29 | | 12:07 | - | 12:50 | 42 | 13:16 | 34 |
| East Croydon | 10.48 | 17 1/2 | 14:01 Sch (14.5) | 0 | 14:47 | 30 | 15:15 | 41 |
| South Croydon | 11.35 | | 2:01 | - | 15:59 | 55 | 16:32 | 57 |
| Purley Oaks | 12.54 | | 3:18 | 54 | - | - | 17:45 | 62 |
| Purley | 13.46 | | 4:14 | 58 | 18:17 | 54 | 18:32 | 62 |
| Coulsdon North | 14.93 | 23 | 5:42 | 61 | 20 | 42* | Tsr | 30 |
| Star Lane | 16.90 | | 7:50 | 56 | 22:25 | 56 | 22:14 | 32 |
| Quarry Tunnel South | 18.60 | | - | - | 24:11 | 59 | - | - |
| Earlswood | 21.81 | 30 | 13:16 | 42 | 27:29 | 52* | 28:57 | 50* |
| Salfords | 23.69 | | 14:58 | 74 | 29:21 | 66 | - | 81 |
| Horley | 25.94 | | - | - | 31:18 | 71 | 32:33 | 80 |
| Gatwick Airport | 26.75 | | 17:31 | 71 | 32:02 | 69 | 33:13 | 79 |
| Three Bridges | 29.44 | 37 | 19:48 | 69 | 34:23 | 68 | 35:20 | 73 |
| Balcombe Tunnel Junction | 31.86 | 39 | 21:53 | 66 | 36:31 | 67 | 37:21 | 70/75 |
| Balcombe | 34.00 | | 23:47 | 68 | 38:27 | 66 | 39:10 | 72 |
| Copyhold Junction | 36.73 | [1] | - | - | 40:55 | 65 | - | - |
| Haywards Heath | 37.91 | 45 | 28:12 tsr | 15 | 42:02 | 62 | 42:30 | 66 |
| Wivelsfield | 40.83 | 48 1/2 | 32:01 | 60 | 44:54 tsr | 60 20 | 45:14 | 60 |
| Burgess Hill | 41.66 | | 32:48 | 66 | 46:38 | 20 | 46:05 | 54 |
| Hassocks | 43.69 | [1] | 34:30 | 69 | 49:46 | 61 | 48:05 | 65 |
| Clayton Tunnel South | 46.01 | | 36:39 | 72 | 51:56 | 68 | 50:14 | 67/74 |
| Patcham Tunnel South | 48.01 | | - | - | 53:38 | 73 | | sigs |
| Preston Park | 49.43 | | 39:42 | - | 54:51 | 66 | 53:40 | 41 |
| BRIGHTON | 50.71 | 60 | 42:58 (Sch 42.5) | - | 57:23 | | 56:25 | |

Table 3: Up runs (Brighton-Victoria), comparing BEL and CIG/BIG stock
(post-July 1967, 55-minute schedule)
(tsr = temporary speed restriction; sigs = signals; sch = schedule; * speed-restricted location)

| Run | | | 6 | | 7 | |
|---|---|---|---|---|---|---|
| Date | | | 16.9.67 | | 6.5.78 | |
| Train | | | 17:45 | | 16:45 | |
| Stock | | | BEL | | CIG/BIG | |
| Units | | | 3052/3053 | | 7427/7040/7304 | |
| Vehicles/Weight (empty)/Weight (full) | | | 10/498/520 | | 12/457/480 | |
| Recorder | | | M.Barrett | | B.Nathan | |
| Timing point | Miles | Schedule (min) | Min:sec | Speed (mph) | Min:sec | Speed (mph) |
| BRIGHTON | 0 | 0 | - | - | - | - |
| Preston Park | 1.29 | | 2:47 | 45 | 2:04 | 57 |
| Patcham Tnl Nth | 2.70 | | - | - | 3:30 | 61 |
| Clayton Tnl Sth | 4.70 | | 6:27 | 61 | 5:24 | 65 |
| Hassocks | 7.03 | | 8:25 | 80 | 7:20 | 78 |
| Burgess Hill | 9.03 | | 10:00 | 72 | 8:52 | 82 |
| Wivelsfield | 9.80 | | 10:43 | 67 | 9:28 | 78 |
| Haywards Heath | 12.80 | 12 | 13:24 tsr | 69 27 | 11:39 | 77 |
| Copyhold Jc | 13.99 | | - | - | 121:36 | 73 |
| Balcombe | 16.71 | | 18:07 | 42 | 15:14 | 54 |
| Balcombe Tnl Jc | 18.85 | | - | - | 17:51 | 62 |
| Three Bridges | 21.26 | | 22:44 | 74 | 19:52 | 79 |
| Gatwick Airport | 23.94 | | 24:58 | 69 | 21:51 | 83 |
| Horley | 24.78 | | 25:42 | 74 | 22:28 | 82 |
| Salfords | 27.03 | | - | - | 24:10 | 76 |
| Earlswood | 28.90 | | 29:20 | 50* | 25:50 | 57* |
| Quarry Tnl Sth | 32.11 | | - | - | 28:52 | 69 |
| Star Lane | 33.81 | | 34:24 | 63 | 30:28 | 59 |
| Coulsdon Nth | 35.79 | | 36:30 | 47* | 32:34 | 53* |
| Purley | 37.25 | | 38:01 | 68 | 33:56 | 67 |
| Purley Oaks | 38.18 | | 38:55 | 65 | sigs | |
| South Croydon | 39.36 | | 40:00 sigs | 50 | 36:26 | 30 |
| East Croydon | 40.24 | 37.5 | 41:25 | 22* | 38:31 | 20* |
| Selhurst | 41.43 | | Dead stand, diversion via slow line, 10 minutes late at Vic (64:15) | | 40:43 | 50 |
| Thornton Heath | 42.15 | | | | - | - |
| Norbury | 43.35 | | | | 42:52 | 58 |
| Streatham Common | 44.21 | | | | 43:46 | 55 |
| Balham | 46.15 | | | | 46:08 | 45 |
| Wandsworth Common | 46.74 | | | | 46:52 | 48 |
| Clapham Jc | 48.11 | | | | 48:44 | 41 |
| Battersea Park | 49.59 | | | | 51:00 | - |
| VICTORIA | 50.71 | 55 | | | 53:56 | - |

Table 4: Down runs (Victoria-Brighton), comparing BEL and CIG/BIG stock
(post-July 1967, 55-minute schedule)
(tsr = temporary speed restriction; sigs = signals; sch = schedule; * speed-restricted location)

| Run | | | 8 | | 9 | |
|---|---|---|---|---|---|---|
| Date | | | 16.8.63 | | 6.5.78 | |
| Train | | | 15:00 | | 15:00 | |
| Stock | | | BEL | | CIG/BIG | |
| Units | | | 3051/3053 | | 7040/7304/7427 | |
| Vehicles/Weight (empty)/Weight (full) | | | 10/498/520 | | 12/457/480 | |
| Recorder | | | D.Benn | | B.Nathan | |
| Timing point | Miles | Schedule (min) | Min:sec | Speed (mph) | Min:sec | Speed (mph) |
| VICTORIA | 0.00 | 0 | 0:00 | - | 0:00 | - |
| Battersea Park | 1.13 | | 2:52 | 45 | 2:50 | - |
| Clapham Junction | 2.60 | | 4:42 | 56 | 4:59 | 51 |
| Wandsworth Common | 3.98 | | 6:09 | 47 | 6:30 | 58 |
| Balham | 4.56 | | 7:08 | 46 | 7:11 | 46* |
| Streatham Common | 6.50 | | 8:54 | 66 | 9:25 | 64 |
| Norbury | 7.36 | | 9:42 | 66 | 10:13 | 64 |
| Selhurst | 9.29 | | 11:29 | 42 | 12:02 | 60 |
| East Croydon | 10.48 | 13 | 13:07 | 43 | 13:31 | 40* |
| South Croydon | 11.35 | | 14:14 | 56 | 14:38 | 52 |
| Purley Oaks | 12.54 | | 15:27 | 60 | - | - |
| Purley | 13.46 | | 16:19 | 61 | 16:44 | 67 |
| Coulsdon North | 14.93 | | 17:51 | 56 | 18:05 | 64 |
| Star Lane | 16.90 | | 19:56 | 60 | 19:54 | 66 |
| Quarry Tunnel South | 18.60 | | 21:32 | 77 | 21:24 | 70 |
| Earlswood | 21.81 | | 24:14 | 63 | 24:23 | 54* |
| Salfords | 23.69 | | 25:50 | 78 | 26:05 | 75 |
| Horley | 25.94 | | 27:33 | 82 | 27:50 | 79 |
| Gatwick Airport | 26.75 | 28 | 28:10 | 80 | 28:29 | 76 |
| Three Bridges | 29.44 | | 30:20 | 76 | 30:37 | 74 |
| Balcombe Tunnel Junction | 31.86 | | 32:25 | 68 | 32:40 | 66 |
| Balcombe | 34.00 | | 34:11 | 81 | 34:29 | 73 |
| Copyhold Junction | 36.73 | | 36:09 | 81 | 36:45 | 69 |
| Haywards Heath | 37.91 | 38 | 37:00 | 82 | 37:47 sigs | 69 |
| Wivelsfield | 40.83 | | 40:17 tsr | 22 | 40:50 | 45 |
| Burgess Hill | 41.66 | | 41:19 | 64 | 41:47 | 60 |
| Hassocks | 43.69 | | 43:21 | 65 | 43:40 | 70 |
| Clayton Tunnel South | 46.01 | | 45:31 | 68 | 45:43 | 65 |
| Patcham Tunnel South | 48.01 | | 47:08 | 76 | 47:31 | 68 |
| Preston Park | 49.43 | | 48:14 | | 48:47 | 65 |
| BRIGHTON | 50.71 | 55 | 51:10 | | 51:18 | - |

Recovery Time in square brackets []

Looking at both Up and Down runs, it is immediately apparent that both BEL and PUL/PAN stock were easily in control of their 60-minute schedule. In Run 1, the Belle ambled up to London at no more than 64, but, after adverse signals at East Croydon, the speed-restricted London suburbs did not allow time to be regained and she was a few minutes late into Victoria. The PUL/PAN performance shown in Run 2 indicated that some harder running up to 79mph was needed to gain time to compensate for a temporary speed restriction at Haywards Heath but, after that, it was a stroll to a right-time arrival at the London terminus. In the Down direction, all three types of stock easily kept within schedule, although one gets the impression that the driver of the CIG/BIG service could not resist 'notching up' his new toy to reach 81mph on the Earlswood-Balcombe Tunnel racing stretch!

Runs detailing the Belle's performance after the July 1967 accelerations have been harder to find but it is very apparent that the old ladies had to pick their skirts up and run! There is no doubt that they could do it. Run 8 is actually a test run, just to see what they were capable of. And the answer was, quite a lot, with Brighton reached in 51 minutes after sustained high-speed running on the racing stretch, much of it at 80mph-plus. One dreads to think of the state of the table linen with all that coffee slopping about, but this is the fastest documented run with BEL stock. The Cigs could do this effortlessly, and provided there were no adverse signals or temporary speed restrictions, the 55-minute schedule was a doddle for them. In the Up direction, some harder running was required from both old and new stock but time could be kept. Even with the severe problem the Belle faced in Run 6, arrival was only 10 minutes late and, as far as East Croydon, she was doing fine. In all runs, the extra p:w ratio available to the BELs and PUL/PAN units over their CIG/BIG successors is apparent in the slightly-faster acceleration away from speed restrictions, particularly at Balham. However, the CIGs could do 90mph and had lower rolling resistance, while the older girls were restricted to 75, so higher maxima were more easily obtained with the CIGs.

So, the BEL units had what they needed to keep to both the 60- and 55-minute schedules with ease, plus that bit more to use if delayed (unless between East Croydon and Victoria, where line speeds and traffic density did not allow it). Higher speeds were just not required and, given the BEL's bogies, the trackwork would be rather uncomfortable. In any case, who really wanted to save a few minutes when savouring the opulence and comfort of a trip on the Brighton Belle?

This chapter would not have been possible without the provision of numerous logs (over 50 from an archive of 258,000) provided by members of the Railway Performance Society (RPS) and their magazine Milepost. If you are interested in the RPS, please contact the RPS Membership Secretary – Peter Smith, 28 Downsview Avenue, Storrington, West Sussex RH20 4PS, www.railperf.org.uk

Speed restricted locations – 50mph – Coulsdon North. The Belle is passing Coulsdon North signal-box and is just diverging on to the through (Quarry) lines. The local (Redhill) lines diverge to the right of the picture. To the left, beyond the signal box, the local lines to Coulsdon North are glimpsed. Two of these continued through the station and rejoined the Quarry line, with a 20mph speed restriction, just south of the junction shown above. These local lines were frequently used by the Belle due to congestion in the East Croydon/Windmill Bridge Junction area. *John Scrace*

Between the steep chalk cuttings on the Quarry Line, near Merstham Tunnel in the early days. A good burst of speed was attainable between the speed restricted junctions at Earlswood and Coulsdon North. *Lens of Sutton*

An Up Brighton Belle service passes Horley on 16th July 1969. The almost dead straight section between Earlswood and Balcombe Tunnel Junction is the fastest stretch of the Brighton line and has often been used for speed and braking trials with various locos and EMUs. *John Scrace*

# Chapter 16
# Last Rites

With the news that the Belle was to be withdrawn, a number of special workings were arranged for enthusiasts and well-wishers to take a final, nostalgic journey. In these last months of service with British Rail, the three 5 BEL units reached places that had never seen a Pullman, let alone the Brighton Belle! On the 1st April 1972, the Railway Correspondence and Travel Society (RCTS) ran a very complex special with 5 BEL unit 3053. This tour was repeated, along exactly the same routes, the following week (8th April). Departing from Waterloo around 10.00am, the RCTS special headed round the Hounslow loop then onwards to Portsmouth Harbour via Chertsey, Woking and Havant. Following reversal at Portsmouth, 3053 headed east to Bognor Regis and Littlehampton, then up the mid-Sussex line via Horsham to Three Bridges. Another reversal took the train to Ore via Lewes and Eastbourne, then steps were retraced to Lewes to allow a trip down the Seaford branch with the obligatory diversion into Newhaven Marine. Finally, the tour headed for Brighton via Falmer to finish with a fast run back to Victoria (57 minutes) along the Belle's usual route, arriving about 7.20pm.

One of the RCTS rail tours visits Waterloo. *John Scrace*

Save the Belle! A young protester makes his feelings known at Brighton on 30th April 1972 in front of the SEG tour train. *Clinton Shaw*

An invitation to the funeral. British Rail cashes in on the Belle's last day. *Clinton Shaw*

The Post Office produced a final day cover to commemorate the Belle's demise with proceeds going to the Southern Railwaymen's home for children and old people, Woking, Surrey. *John Scrace Collection*

John Bradshaw trading as JB Photocards produced 500 commemorative phonecards in conjunction with BT and agreement from BR for use of the 150 Years of the Brighton Line logo.

*Ring out the Belle and let it rest*
*In some fair haven of the blest.*
*Dull logic turned aghast aside*
*From Pullmans for such short a ride,*
*But here, in shaded lamplight's gleam*
*The airy fabric of a dream*
*Sustained by kippers, toast and tea*
*Could reach the heights of fantasy.*
*A dragon, legendary beast,*
*Cropped at the grass at Croydon (East)*
*And bashful wood nymphs, hard to coax,*
*Hid in the trees at Purley Oaks.*
*All this – and more – at low expense;*
*The supplement was thirty pence.*
*Anon.*

Goodbye Belle! 3051 on the 'Cheese and Wine' special on 30th April 1972. *John Scrace*

Following reversal at Three Bridges, the SEG special headed down the mid-Sussex line via Horsham, arriving at Littlehampton.
*Clinton Shaw*

On Sunday 30th April, the final day of regular services, crowds thronged the lineside between London and Brighton to get a last glimpse of this famous train. Four return services were run, plus a 'Cheese and Wine' and late night 'Champagne Special'. On the same day, the Southern Electric Group (SEG) ran another, less complex railtour from Brighton employing unit 3051. As the special awaited departure, units 3052/3 arrived at Brighton at 12.00 on the 11.00 service from Victoria, giving the rare sight of all three BEL units at the same location. The SEG special left Brighton at 12.20 for Three Bridges, reversing there and heading via Horsham to Littlehampton then on to Bognor Regis. After returning to Three Bridges (with an extended photo-stop at Christ's Hospital), it reversed again and took the Newhaven Boat Train route via Keymer Junction and Lewes to Newhaven Harbour, then back via Falmer to arrive at Brighton at 16.47, in time for the 17.45 Belle departure back to London.

After the SEG railtour, 3051 waited at Brighton while 3052/3 headed back to Victoria on the regular 17.45 service train. On arrival at the capital, 3053 worked the 19.00 return to Brighton, 20.45 return to Victoria and 22.00 final service train to Brighton. Meanwhile, 3051 formed a special 'Cheese and Wine' run from Brighton to Victoria where it coupled to 3052 for a historic 'Champagne Special', leaving London at 22.30 and crawling into Brighton at 23.52 to be greeted by the Haywards Heath Silver Band playing 'Auld Lang Syne' and 'Land of Hope and Glory' and hordes of well-wishers. As in life, so in death, the Brighton Belle passed into history on a wave of food and drink, consumed in luxury surroundings!

5 BEL units 3052 and 3053 ran empty to Victoria on 3rd May 1972 for the removal of dry stores and equipment, later returning to Brighton Lovers' Walk depot. 3051 made one more passenger-carrying trip on 9th May in association with that year's Brighton Festival and the following day it too made a round trip to Victoria for stores' removal. The units were then split up and five of the motor coaches (all except 289) were moved to Selhurst depot for the removal of any electrical equipment that could be useful to BR for maintaining its remaining pre-war stock.

Above right: After reversal at Bognor, the SEG special headed for Three Bridges for the second time. An extended photo-stop was taken at Christ's Hospital, with an opportunity for the tour's participants and Pullman attendants to parade in their finery. *Clinton Shaw*

Right: Absolutely the last one – at least for the next 40 years. Unit 3051 heads empty for Victoria for its final passenger duty on 9th May 1972. *Clinton Shaw*

# Chapter 17
# The Belle Preserved

As is usual with withdrawn rolling stock, BR offered the Brighton Belle fleet for sale by auction. Normally the bidders were specialist scrap metal dealers but, with the growth of interest in railway history during the 1960 and 1970s, commercial organisations and groups of enthusiasts would also occasionally bid for unusual or historically significant vehicles. Remarkably, all 15 Belle cars were preserved in one form or another and all but one, which was subsequently destroyed by fire, still exist today.

At first sight it seems surprising that the railway preservation movement, which had its origins in saving Welsh narrow-gauge lines in the 1950s and had graduated to restoring standard gauge branch railways such as the Bluebell Line, was not more strongly represented among the original bidders for the iconic Brighton Belle cars in 1972. However these heritage railways were, and largely still are, focused on steam haulage and the work involved in converting a former electric multiple unit car for this purpose is considerable. Vehicle-end gangways and couplings must be adapted or replaced. The Westinghouse air brake system must be stripped out and replaced by vacuum brake equipment. Electric heating must be removed and replaced with steam heating pipes and radiators. The 70V lighting circuits have to be re-wired for a 24V electricity supply from an underfloor battery and an axle-driven dynamo with a regulator and through-lighting control.

Back in 1972, there was a plentiful supply of redundant vacuum-braked, steam-heated BR rolling stock and an impoverished preserved railway could buy a complete set of coaches and put it into revenue-earning service for less cost and time than was required to purchase and adapt a single Brighton Belle car.

Restoration and adaptation of EMU stock for locomotive haulage can be done – in 1990 the Bluebell Railway's carriage works staff did a beautiful job of restoring and converting one of the Belle's sisters, 'Bertha', a Pullman composite car from one of the Southern's 6 PUL Brighton Line express units – but the task is not for the faint-hearted or the underfunded.

Many of the Brighton Belle cars were originally sold to breweries to be used as pub restaurants, capitalising on the association with Pullman catering. Six of these, Trailer Parlour Thirds 285, 286, 287 and Driving Motor Brake Parlour Thirds 291, 292 and 293 were purchased by Allied Breweries. They

First Class Kitchen car no. 279 'Hazel' at the Black Bull Inn, Moulton, North Yorkshire. *Black Bull Inn*

Driving Motor Brake Parlour Third no. 289 as 'The Derbyshire Belle' motel. *Little Mill Inn*

were briefly moved to Mistley in Essex from August 1972, then to a longer-term stay in a siding at nearby Manningtree, adjacent to the GER main line between London and Norwich. One of the authors remembers seeing them from his regular trips between Norwich and Liverpool Street in 1975 when a student at the University of East Anglia. It certainly made him look twice! Driving Motor Brake Parlour Third no. 288 went to Truman Breweries and Trailer Kitchen First no. 281 (formerly 'Gwen') to Whitbread. In addition, Trailer Kitchen Firsts 279 ('Hazel'), 283 ('Mona') and Driving Motor Brake Parlour Third no. 289 went to inns in Yorkshire, Cheshire and Derbyshire respectively. But priorities change rapidly in the pub and restaurant industry and, as early as 1973, some of these cars were being sold or loaned to preserved railways. This process has continued and today (2011) only two 'Belle' cars, 279 and 289, are still owned by innkeepers:

### 279 'Hazel'

Trailer Kitchen First no. 279 from unit 3051 was sold to Audrey and George Pagendam after withdrawal from BR service and went north by rail to Darlington on the 26th July 1972, then on by road to her new role as a restaurant at the Black Bull Inn in Moulton, North Yorkshire.

Her owners have since had her refurbished and restored her to a very high standard, reinstating her original Pullman umber and cream livery and name, 'Hazel'. She has become a very special part of the Black Bull, now owned by Phillip Barker, and is still doing today what she has always done best – serving good food in stylish surroundings. See www.blackbullmoulton.com for more details.

### 289

Driving Motor Brake Parlour Third no. 289, also from unit 3051, was sold to Mr D. N. Clay and moved from Brighton on the 14th June 1972 by rail to Stockport, continuing by road to her destination, the Little Mill Inn at Rowarth, Cheshire, on the 23rd June 1972. She was 'relocated' again in 1974 when county border changes placed Rowarth in Derbyshire.

Once ensconced in her new home, 289 was given a repaint into umber and cream Pullman livery and was later renamed 'The Derbyshire Belle'. She was used as a restaurant until mid-1985 but in 1986 her interior was reconfigured into three en-suite bedrooms, retaining the original wood and brass fittings, and she is now marketed as the Derbyshire Belle Motel. See www.thelittlemill.co.uk for more details.

### 290

Driving Motor Brake Parlour Third no. 290 was the unlucky one and is the only car of the original 15 that is no longer with us. She was initially purchased by British Transport Hotels and left Brighton for restoration as Car no. 90 at Wolverton Works in Buckinghamshire on the 26th November 1972. Between 1980 and 1990 she was used in passenger service on the Nene Valley Railway based at Wansford, Cambridgeshire, sometimes paired with 3142, the Southern Electric Group's vintage electric multiple unit. Sold on, she was initially moved to Padiham power station near Burnley where her condition deteriorated rapidly. Bill Black and Peter Watkinson bought her in April 1991 and took her to Carnforth for a five-year project to restore her as a locomotive-hauled Pullman Parlour Brake.

As part of the restoration process, during the afternoon of 18th July that year, hot work was carried out on her and in the early hours of the following morning someone standing on Carnforth station platform saw flames coming from the Steamtown site. By this time she was well ablaze and was gutted before the fire could be put out. A final attempt to restore Car 90 was made at the East Lancashire Railway at Bury, Lancashire, but she was further fire damaged by vandals and left beyond repair. Eventually, her sad remains were disposed of for scrap, and Car 90 was cut up at Bury during 1995.

# Chapter 18
# The Belle on the Orient Express

The Orient Express Wagons Lits service from Paris to Istanbul started operations in the 1880s. When the 12½-mile long Simplon Tunnel through the Alps was opened in 1919, a variant of the service, the 'Simplon-Orient Express' was routed via Lausanne, Milan, Verona, Trieste, Belgrade and Sofia. Between the first and second world wars the service was a byword for luxury travel, romance and intrigue, first captured in Graham Greene's 1932 novel 'Stamboul Train' and two years later by Agatha Christie's detective story 'Murder on the Orient Express'.

By the 1950s the service was facing stiff competition from airlines but its its aura of glamour and excitement was boosted by Ian Fleming's 1957 novel 'From Russia with Love' and the Terence Young 1963 film of the same name, in which much of the action takes place on the train. However it was Sidney Lumet's sumptuous 1974 film adaptation of Agatha Christie's novel that most strongly evoked the Orient Express in its heyday. In reality the Orient Express was by now a pale shadow of its former self, patronised largely by migrant workers, students and backpackers.

'Audrey', with tables laid up for dinner on the VSOE. *SEG Collection*

It was when the remaining former Orient Express Wagons-Lits cars were auctioned off that James B Sherwood, founder and chairman of the Sea Containers group of companies, launched a £10m project to re-create the Orient Express of the 1920s and 1930s, using meticulously restored vintage rolling stock. This *train de luxe* service, which commenced in 1982 and is still running successfully today under the name of the Venice Simplon-Orient Express (VSOE), consists of two elements: a British Pullman train between London Victoria and Folkestone (where passengers transit the Channel Tunnel by coach) and a Wagons-Lits day/sleeping car service onwards from Calais to Paris and Venice. George Mortimer Pullman would certainly have approved! The British Pullman is made up of cars from a wide range of sources, including former Brighton Belle First Class kitchen cars 'Audrey', 'Vera' and 'Gwen' and, apart from its VSOE duties, is used for charters and special trains and a weekly dining trip from Victoria.

## 280 'Audrey'

Trailer Kitchen First 280 from unit 3052 was bought by Mr David Lowther and moved to the Ashford Steam Centre on the 19th June 1972. Sea Containers Ltd bought the car in 1980, taking her to the Steamtown railway heritage site at Carnforth for restoration as 'Audrey', during which fragments of shrapnel were found still embedded in her marquetry panelling from her 1940 encounter with the Luftwaffe.

'Audrey' is also a film star! In her Orient Express role she featured in 'Bullseye', a 1990 comedy with sequences filmed on the Mid Hants Railway. Produced and directed by Michael Winner, and starring Michael Caine and Roger Moore, Audrey's silver screen debut failed to be nominated for an Oscar. In fact a review in *Time Out* described the film as a 'stinker'. Though still awaiting another call from her agent 'Audrey' has since been superbly restored and is now operating as part of the VSOE's British Pullman train.

'Audrey' at Folkestone Harbour on the VSOE, 21st June 2007. As this branch has now closed, the VSOE scheduled service terminates at Folkestone East. *David Glasspool*

'Gwen' at Folkestone Harbour on the VSOE, 21st June 2007. *David Glasspool*

## 281 'Gwen'

Trailer Kitchen First 281 from unit 3053 was still languishing at Brighton in January 1974. Her original buyer sold her on to Whitbread Breweries, and she was used at the 'Horseless Carriage Inn', Chingford Hatch, Essex, as a restaurant where she was nicely restored to Pullman umber-and-cream livery under her original name 'Gwen' and with lots of Pullman memorabilia. The end gangways were removed and the seating changed to 2+1 formation for her pub role.

In 1981, she went to the Colne Valley Railway, Castle Hedingham in Essex. The intention was that she would be used as part of their dining train. However the conversion was limited to fitting a vacuum through-pipe rather than full vacuum brakes and she was only occasionally hauled by a locomotive and was principally used as a static venue for cream teas. In 1988, VSOE Ltd made the Colne Valley Railway a very good offer; to exchange two locomotive-hauled Pullman cars, 'Aquila' and Car No. 36, for 'Gwen'. 'Gwen' was moved to the VSOE depot at Stewarts Lane, Battersea, where she was fully restored and, in March 1999, she joined 'Audrey' and 'Vera' in the British Pullman train.

## 283 'Mona'

Trailer Kitchen First 283 was initially moved from Brighton to Slough on the 7th July 1972. She was briefly based at Thorpe Park, Chertsey, then at the nearby Eastley End Restaurant before moving in April 1974 to the Brighton Belle Inn (previously the Railway Inn), at Winsford in Cheshire. After 24 years as a restaurant, she was sold to VSOE Ltd in April 1998 and is now stored at Stewarts Lane as part of the reserve fleet.

## 284 'Vera'

Trailer Kitchen First 284 was originally sold to Mr Anedee Turner and was taken by low loader to the large garden of his private residence at Westleton, Suffolk. In 1988 she was sold to Sea Containers Ltd who carried out a full renovation to their usual superb standard, reinstating her original umber and cream livery and restoring her original name, 'Vera'.

She entered service in the VSOE British Pullman set from August 1990 and, in September 1991, 'Vera' and 'Audrey' (with other VSOE Pullman cars) took part in a re-creation of the 'Brighton Belle' to celebrate the 150th anniversary of the London to Brighton line.

## 286

Trailer Parlour Third no. 286 was one of the 'Allied Breweries Six' and, after leaving Brighton on the 29th June 1972, spent nearly three years in that siding in Manningtree, before moving on to York on the 18th May 1975, then to Steamtown, Carnforth, now in the ownership of Sea Containers Limited. Restoration was started at Carnforth but 1986 found Car 286 at Swindon and she is now at Stewarts Lane, as part of the VSOE reserve fleet.

## 292 and 293

Two more of the 'Allied Breweries Six', Driving Motor Brake Parlour Thirds 292 and 293 from unit 3053, were in the train that left Brighton on the 24th July 1972 for Mistley and were then moved on to Manningtree. However in September of that year, Cars 292 and 293 were resold to the Brighton Museum of Transport, which was to have been located in the old Pullman Car works at Preston Park, and the two Belle cars were moved back to their old home. Due to lack of funding, the museum project never got off the ground and the concept was abandoned from mid-1994. 292 and 293 deteriorated badly in the now-closed works and were badly vandalised. Eventually, all the locos were dispersed and, following removal of the remaining stock on Sunday 7th September 2008, the old Pullman Works was closed and demolished.

Meanwhile, the VSOE had an operating problem. Each time the British Pullman set is used, a second locomotive is needed just to move the train a couple of miles between its depot at Stewarts Lane and the platform at Victoria. VSOE bought 292 and 293 with a view to converting them to driving trailer cars, with staff accommodation and baggage space, so enabling the set to be propelled to and from the depot by a single locomotive at the rear.

On April 20th 2005, both cars set sail for the RSI (formerly Wagons-Lits) workshops in Ostend, Belgium for restoration. Some progress was made with Car 292 – the bodysides were shot blasted and painted in primer but then RSI went out of business and both cars were returned to Stewarts Lane where they ponder their future. VSOE has kindly donated the redundant traction electrical equipment from 293 to the Southern Electric Group to assist in the restoration of 3142, its vintage Southern Electric express unit.

Opposite top: The VSOE Pullman train arrives at Brighton on Saturday 21st September 1991 to take part in the Brighton 150 celebrations. The train includes ex-Belle cars 'Audrey' and 'Vera' and is hauled by Class 73 loco, 'Brighton Evening Argus', in Pullman livery. *Brian Morrison*

Opposite left: Car (2)92 in appalling condition at Preston Park Pullman Works in 1996. *Ian Morgan*

Opposite right: Car 292 is seen in the RSI works in Ostend under restoration and conversion to a driving trailer. *VSOE*

# Chapter 19
# The Belle Reborn?

As commercial enterprises lost interest in their Belle purchases, individual cars would be loaned or sold to a preserved railway then, once the immensity of the task became apparent, they were moved on again. Many of the Belle cars have spent considerable periods in open air storage in this way and, because of the consequent deterioration, their subsequent restoration has proved all the more difficult.

The 'third wave' of Belle preservation is much more positive and encouraging. The purchase and meticulous restoration of cars for the Venice Simplon-Orient Express service was described in the previous chapter. More recently, the Transport Trust, a national charity dedicated the preservation and restoration of Britain's transport heritage, has launched an exciting plan to recreate a fully-operational 5-car Brighton Belle unit.

As he conducted research for his book charting the progress of railway preservation in Britain, Denis Dunstone, a trustee and a member of the Transport Trust's Council, realised that the electric train had received scant attention. The basic infrastructure did not exist, with no heritage railway having invested in either third rail or overhead electricity supply; further, the electric train was now so commonplace that it lacked some of the romantic appeal of steam.

He noted that, while a handful of important and well-preserved examples were held by the NRM and London Transport, projects undertaken by private individuals to collect, restore and preserve electric trains had suffered from a shortage of funds and the absence of prioritisation of artefacts for preservation. His conclusion was that, unless steps were taken as matter of urgency to highlight the importance of the electric train to Britain's rail heritage, many key elements could end up as scrap. What was needed was a restoration programme that would capture the imagination of a broad swathe of the public and raise the profile – and status – of the electric train.

The Transport Trust is the only heritage organisation with a complete overview of transport preservation and it had been aware for some time of the position of electric train preservation. Dunstone persuaded the Trust that the key to unlocking latent support for electric train preservation was to revive the iconic Brighton Belle and return it to the main line. A project of this scale and vision would act as a catalyst for further electric preservation.

The Trust was aware of the location and condition of the remaining fourteen Brighton Belle carriages that were now scattered around Scotland, Yorkshire, Derbyshire and London. After further research and many conversations with owners, the Trust determined that assembling a train set was feasible; most critically, two Driving Motor Thirds – the most recognisable of the set – were available, together with two trailers. Four out of five would be enough to be going on with!

In January 2009 the 5BEL Trust was established as an independent charitable trust to acquire and own these four carriages, to raise money for their restoration and to operate them and others as a train. After a very long year of detailed negotiations and planning, the Brighton Belle project was launched at the National Railway Museum, York, in July 2009 and a special steam train bearing the headboard 'Brighton Belle' and hauled by preserved Gresley A4 Pacific steam locomotive 'Bittern' ran non-stop to London.

The event appeared symbolic of the growing recognition that the time for electric rail preservation had arrived. For their part, the 5BEL Trustees set themselves the target of restoring to a professional standard a minimum of three cars – Driving Motor Brake Thirds 88 and 91 and one of Trailer Thirds 85 and 87 – by 2012. As and when funds donated by the public permit, the Trust intends to restore the other trailer.

The 5BEL Trust has set itself the considerable challenge of making the restored train fit to run on the electrified main lines and is working with a specialised engineering consultancy to ensure that the unit will comply with all of the mandatory requirements for operation on the 21st century railway – no light matter for vehicles built in 1932! Fortunately, the strong, rigid all-steel construction of the 5 BEL cars goes some way towards meeting modern safety standards – in fact they are stronger than vehicles built as recently as the 1970s! However, the original screw couplings between the intermediate Belle cars offer no protection against 'telescoping' – one vehicle crushing the body of another in a collision. The gangways will be retained but the couplings must be replaced by something that meets today's Railway Group Standards, such as a buckeye coupler with override protection, as used by the VSOE fleet. This will render the original buffers redundant, though these distinctive features will be retained *in situ* if possible.

Car 88 undergoing bodywork restoration at Ramparts, Derby in October 2009. *5BEL Trust*

The traction motors, switchgear and cab controls were removed for scrap by British Rail and replacements must be acquired from other electric multiple units or manufactured from scratch. As described in Chapter 6, each motor coach has two power bogies with two traction motors – eight motors per unit. The original Metrovick motors were replaced by English Electric EE163 units in 1955 but neither of these types is available today.

The project will therefore use eight of the rugged, reliable EE507 250hp traction motors that were fitted to post-war SR suburban electric multiple units right up to 1990. These motors have type-approval for use on Network Rail and many are still in front line service with Southern and South West Trains. Compatible, type-approved traction control equipment will be sourced from redundant electric multiple unit stock – the project has already recovered four traction motors and a complete set of camshaft control gear from withdrawn 4 CIG 1881 – ironically one of the Belle's successors on the Brighton line.

The Trust thought long and hard before breaking up the 4 CIG unit but in fact very little material will be wasted. The unit's trailer saloon is being donated intact to the Dean Forest Railway to enable them to complete their 4 CIG unit No. 1499 whilst components from other cars such as doors, windows, seating and fittings will be donated to preserved railways with CIG and other BR Mark 1 vehicles. The restored Brighton Belle unit will also need to have modern 'black box' on-train monitoring equipment, new auxiliary electrical circuitry for normal and emergency lighting, and possibly for catering, and a new air braking system. A secondary door locking system, controlled by the traincrew, is now required for all trains with passenger-operated doors. The VSOE company has developed a safe system of operation for its British Pullman set, which includes ex-Belle cars, and this will be adopted for the project.

It is possible that the original two-plus-two seating arrangement of the Third Class cars, which was always a bit cramped, will be converted to two-plus-one, requiring a rebuild of seating and tables. The two-plus-one arrangement will permit not only silver service of meals, but will also help the train meet the requirements of disabled passengers.

## 288

Driving Motor Brake Third no. 288 is the first vehicle to form part of the Transport Trust's plan to recreate a 5 BEL unit, and in October 2008, she was moved to Rampart C&W works in Derby to complete her restoration as Car No. 88. Originally in unit 3051, Car No. 288 was purchased from British Rail by Truman Breweries and moved from Norwood Yard to Temple Mills Yard in east London on the 14th October 1972, then shortly afterwards on to Clacton, Essex, on the 27th October. However her intended use as a restaurant in a Truman pub proved impracticable and she was loaned to the Stour Valley Railway, moving to Chappel & Wakes Colne in Essex on the 5th July 1975.

After a while, 288 was transferred to Stour Valley Railway ownership but this Southern coach did not fit in with the railway's GER/LNER style. Under pressure to free siding space for other preserved vehicles the company agreed to lease 288 to the Southern Steam Trust, then based on the Swanage Railway in Dorset. With a view to using her on the 'Purbeck Pullman' service, the Swanage Railway fitted 288 with vacuum brakes, refurbished the interior and repainted her in umber and cream, though 'Pullman' lettering, lining and the traditional 'Car No. 88 Third Class' lettering were never applied.

In August 1988 the VSOE company purchased 288 for its reserve fleet and moved her to its Stewarts Lane depot where she was stored until her acquisition by the Transport Trust in 2009.

Car 88 is seen hauled by privately preserved Great Western Railway-design pannier tank, 9466, during its spell on the Swanage Railway. *Michael Baker*

Lots to do! Interior of Car 88 at Ramparts works, Derby, October 2009. *5BEL Trust*

Car 88 undergoing bodywork restoration at Ramparts, Derby in October 2009. *5BEL Trust*

## 287 and 291

Trailer Parlour Third No. 287 and Driving Motor Brake Parlour Third No. 291, both from unit 3052 and both members of the 'Allied Brewery Six', left Brighton on the 29th June 1972 via Temple Mills for Mistley, Essex, before joining the other Allied cars in storage on a siding at Manningtree.

After a few years at Manningtree, 287 and 291 were both leased to the North Norfolk Railway (NNR) at Sheringham, Norfolk, arriving there on the 16th March 1975. Both cars were externally restored to Pullman umber-and-cream livery as Cars Nos. 87 and 91 respectively, in the course of which their seats were re-upholstered and the rather awkward arm-rests removed. They were fitted with 240V electricity supplied by a portable generator and used in the NNR's Pullman 'Wine and Dine' trains, although as they retained air brakes, they could only be hauled by a few locomotives.

During their stay on the NNR, cars 87 and 91 featured in the 1994 BBC TV series 'Love on a Branch Line', based on John Hadfield's 1959 book, in which the eccentric Lord Flamborough (Leslie Phillips) lives on a steam train on a private railway. His home is the two Pullman cars and the railway is the NNR, with Weybourne standing in for Arcady Halt station and Sheringham as Flaxfield station. The British Comedy Guide describes 'Love on a Branch Line' as offering

'… *a brand of gentle post-war escapism not dissimilar to that featured in The Darling Buds of May. Central character Jasper Pye is taken from the drudgery of his everyday city life and transported to a rural paradise. The pleasures of the series can be derived from the beautiful scenery, nostalgic music and from the three beautiful sisters who Jasper comes across'.*

In 2002, the NNR agreed a five-year lease of 87 and 91 to the Keith and Dufftown Railway (KDR), both cars moving north in June of that year. The KDR planned to give both cars a complete refurbishment and to use them on special-hire dining events. However, due to their weight they could not be loco-hauled until certain bridges on the line had been strengthened.

In October 2008 the two companions were separated for the first time in many years when, due to water ingress from a deteriorating roof, Driving Motor Brake Parlour Third no. 91 was moved back from Dufftown to Holt station, on the North Norfolk Railway. Trailer Third No. 87 is still far from her Brighton roots at Dufftown station where she is occasionally used for static dining.

The North Norfolk Railway has assigned ownership of Cars 87 and 91 to the 5BEL Trust and in October 2009, Car No. 91 was moved to Rampart C&W in Derby to become the second Brighton Belle car to undergo restoration to her former glory. She will be joined by No. 87 as soon as space permits.

Cars 91 (front) and 87 (behind) during their stay on the North Norfolk Railway on 21st November 1999.
*Steve Allen*

Interior of Car 91, showing the modifications made by the NNR, including the removal of the armrests. *5BEL Trust*

Cars 91 and 88 are reunited at Ramparts in October 2009. *5BEL Trust*

Car 88 with restored bodywork poses with 'Doris' at Horsted Keynes on 6th August 2010 during a brief visit to the Bluebell Line. She was then taken by road to Bristol Barrow Hill to have 4 CIG motors and running gear fitted and then back to Ramparts at Derby for interior restoration. *Ashley Saunders*

## 285

The last of the 'Allied Brewery Six', Trailer Parlour Third no. 285 from unit 3053, spent a short while at Manningtree before being moved to the the Nag's Head, Mickleover, Derbyshire for use as a restaurant, where she was restored externally to her original, pre-1968 livery as Car no. 85.

In 1993 Scottish & Newcastle Breweries donated Car no. 85, by now without her internal fittings, to the Severn Valley Railway (SVR) who intended to use her as part of their Dining train. This plan was not carried through and, after prolonged storage in the SVR's Arley sidings, she was resold to VSOE Limited in April 1998 and sent to Stewarts Lane to join its reserve fleet. However, the VSOE is focusing on First Class cars for its British Pullman train and now regards Car no. 85 as surplus to its requirements, even attempting to sell the car on the auction website e-bay but failing to reach the reserve price. VSOE has since sold Car no. 85 to the Transport Trust and she is now at Derby, third on the restoration list.

## 282 'Doris' – the fifth car

The original Brighton Belle units each contained two First Class kitchen cars but as we have seen, of the six originals, three, 'Audrey', 'Gwen' and 'Vera', are in the VSOE British Pullman set and a fourth, 'Mona' is in the company's reserve fleet whilst 'Hazel' is a static restaurant in private ownership.

In 1972 BR sold Trailer Kitchen First 282 from unit 3051 to City Industrial Limited, shop-fitters, and she left Brighton on 17th August of that year for Finsbury Park, north London. Early in 1975 she went to Derby for repainting into her original umber and cream livery and reinstatement of her name 'Doris', returning to London in June the same year. For many years, 'Doris' was a familiar sight to travellers on the East Coast Main Line, as she was visible from the platforms on the west side of Finsbury Park station, resplendent in her Pullman livery in the former milk dock. However, during the Christmas 2003 holiday period, she was the victim of a graffiti attack and her condition subsequently gradually deteriorated.

The committee of the Bluebell Railway Preservation Society agreed to a privately-funded project to move 'Doris' and on 9th April 2006 she left north London for her new home. Her Pullman livery was restored and graffiti paint removed from her windows and she was placed in Platform 1 at Horsted Keynes where she has been earning her keep serving cream teas to the public. The original intention had been for 'Doris' to become a much-needed second kitchen car in the Bluebell Railway's all-Pullman 'Golden Arrow' train. However, quite apart from the difficulty and cost of converting an electric multiple unit car for steam haulage, the Bluebell Railway Society recognised that this would permanently alter a vehicle of historic significance. In February 2011 Jim Kay agreed to sell his Pullman kitchen car 'Carina' to the Bluebell Railway. Built in 1951 for the 'Golden Arrow', Carina formed part of Sir Winston Churchill's funeral train on 30th January 1965. Like the 'Belle' cars she later suffered the indignity of being repainted in BR's corporate blue and grey and, since withdrawal from BR service, has passed through the hands of several owners. The Bluebell Railway has taken on the challenge of restoring 'Carina' to her former glory and adding her to their 'Golden Arrow' train and has released 'Doris' to the Transport Trust. The restored Brighton Belle will therefore be a full 5-car unit.

This is a fitting end to this book. The history of the Belle has come full circle. She never really died, just slept for a short while to awake into her new and diverse roles. If the aspirations of the Trust are met, all those who have admired and loved this most iconic of trains will see and travel on the Old Girl as she returns to mainline service in her 80th year. The heritage transport industry has taken on many difficult, even seemingly-impossible, challenges and succeeded. If the commitment and funding is forthcoming, there is no reason why history cannot be made, and the first restored heritage EMU be returned to the mainline. And once one succeeds, it is our fervent hope that others will quickly follow and the Southern rails will once again ring with the distinctive sight and sounds of 1930s EMUs on their home ground.

The coupe in 'Doris' as stabled at Horsted Keynes. *Laurel Arnison*

Car 88 saloon interior before restoration, Horsted Keynes, 6th August 2010. *Ashley Saunders*

# Chapter 20
# The Other Belles

As well as the 15 cars that made up the three 5 BEL units for Brighton Belle services, individual Pullman Kitchen Composite cars were formed into 23 other electric multiple units that operated Southern main line services to Brighton, Eastbourne/Hastings and Worthing/Littlehampton. The 23 all-steel Pullman kitchen cars were built by MCWF and were the first Pullman composites ever built; they were 68ft 9in long, tared 43 tons and had 12 First and 16 Third Class seats. A 20kW dynamotor mounted on the underframe delivered a 110V power supply for the all-electric kitchen. First Class seats were arranged 1+1 and Second Class 2+2 either side of a central gangway and the internal layout was vestibule, 2-bay Third Class saloon, lavatory, 4-seat First Class compartment, 2-bay First Class saloon, pantry, kitchen, vestibule. As with the Belle cars themselves, interiors were sumptuous, ornate and very traditional, with elaborate panelling of hardwood from various parts of the Empire and metalwork finished in 'satin silver'.

Although the cars did, of course, have stock numbers ('schedule' numbers in Pullman parlance) they followed the Pullman practice for First Class cars of displaying names, rather than numbers, prominently on the bodysides. Like the Brighton Belle First Class cars, they carried girls' names that recall the 1930s.

As a result of operating and staffing pressures during the 1939-45 war, Pullman car and other catering services were withdrawn from 22nd May 1942. The Pullman cars were stored and the PUL and CIT units operated as 5COR until 1st May 1946. When the Pullman cars were reinstated on 1st May 1946 most of them returned to their original units. Exceptions were 'Olive' to 3002, 'Gwladys' to 3017, 'Ethel' to 3018, 'May' to 3041, 'Ruth' to 3042 and 'Rita' to 3043. In a subsequent exchange 3001 received 'Bertha', and 'Anne' went to 3012. As the overhauling of SR and Pullman vehicles rarely coincided there were other temporary changes from time to time.

Sadly, most of these Pullman cars were scrapped when the units they operated in were withdrawn in the mid-1960s. However, two were preserved. 'Ruth' is stored as part of the VSOE reserve fleet and 'Bertha' has been restored to a superb standard and operates today on the Swanage Railway.

| 1932 unit no. | 1937 unit no. | Trailer Pullman Kitchen Composite |
|---|---|---|
| 2001 | 3001 | (275) 'Anne' |
| 2002 | 3002 | (256) 'Rita' |
| 2003 | 3003 | (257) 'Grace' |
| 2004 | 3004 | (260) 'Elinor' |
| 2005 | 3005 | (263) 'Ida' |
| 2006 | 3006 | (265) 'Rose' |
| 2007 | 3007 | (266) 'Violet' |
| 2008 | 3008 | (277) 'Lorna' |
| 2009 | 3009 | (271) 'Alice' |
| 2010 | 3010 | (274) 'Daisy' |
| 2011 | 3011 | (276) 'Naomi' |
| 2012 | 3012 | (278) 'Bertha' |
| 2013 | 3013 | (258) 'Brenda' |
| 2014 | 3014 | (259) 'Enid' |
| 2015 | 3015 | (261) 'Joyce' |
| 2016 | 3016 | (262) 'Iris' |
| 2017 | 3017 | (264) 'Ruth' |
| 2018 | 3018 | (267) 'May' |
| 2019 | 3019 | (268) 'Peggy' |
| 2020 | 3020 | (269) 'Clara' |
| 2041 | 3041 | (272) 'Gwladys' |
| 2042 | 3042 | (273) 'Olive' |
| 2043 | 3043 | (270) 'Ethel' |

Pullman car 'Alice' from 6 PUL unit 3009 is seen on the 'PUL/PAN Farewell Tour' organised by the Locomotive Club of Great Britain on Sunday 24th April 1966. These First Class Pullman cars were similar in style and construction to their equivalents in the 5 BEL units. *Clinton Shaw*

Of the non-Pullman cars in these units, the two driving motor cars were all-steel and, like the prototypes described in Chapter 5, were supplied by contractors. Half of the order went to the Birmingham Railway Carriage and Wagon Co. Ltd and half to the Metropolitan-Cammell Carriage Wagon and Finance Co. Ltd. The Southern Railway built the three non-Pullman trailers in each of these units in its own workshops, the steel underframes at Lancing and the wooden-framed, steel-clad bodies at Eastleigh.

Units 2001-2020 seated 72 First and 236 Third (later Second) Class passengers. Units 2041-2043 had 138 First and 124 Third Class seats. A pair originally formed the prestige 8.45am and 5.00pm return 'City Limited' service from Brighton to London Bridge whilst the third operated the 8.30am West Worthing to London Bridge, returning as the rear portion of the 6.04pm service to West Worthing and detaching at Hove. 2001-2020 were originally classified 6 COR and 2041-2043 6 COR* but they were reclassified 6 PUL and 6 CIT in 1936 and were renumbered 3001-3020 and 3041-3043 respectively in January 1937. Following changing traffic patterns, the three 6 CIT units worked the Brighton, Worthing and recently electrified Eastbourne services, usually paired with a 6 PAN or 6 PUL unit. Units 3041 and 3042 each had one of the two prototype motor coaches described in Chapter 5. These had slightly larger saloons and an additional four seats, giving a total of 204 Third Class seats per unit.

Above: First Class saloon of Pullman Composite car 'Anne'. *Doug Lindsay Collection*

Opposite upper: First Class saloon of Pullman Composite car 'Alice'. *Doug Lindsay Collection*

Opposite lower: First Class saloon of Pullman Composite car 'Enid'. *Doug Lindsay Collection*

# Appendix 1

## Some Explanatory Notes

Like any specialist subject, railways have a language of their own. These notes are provided to assist the general reader to understand some of the technical terms used in this book.

'Atlantic', 'Baltic', etc. Frederick Methvan Whyte, an American railroad engineer, devised a system of notation to describe the wheel arrangements of steam locomotives, comprising leading (unpowered) wheels, wheels driven by the engine and trailing (unpowered) wheels. Thus a locomotive that simply had two axles (four wheels) driven by the engine is classified 0-4-0. Some of the configurations acquired shorthand names, often derived from the name of an individual locomotive. For example a 4-4-2 locomotive (two leading axles, two powered axles and one trailing axle) became known as an 'Atlantic'. Locomotives that carried their water supply in tanks rather than in a separate tender carried the suffix 'T'. 'ST' indicated a saddle tank locomotive.

Bogie. Flanged railway wheels have a slightly conical tread profile. This means that a pair of wheels rigidly fixed to an axle are more or less self-steering as they roll along the rails and the flanges only come into contact with the sides of the rails on very sharp curves. To enable the wheels of a long vehicle to follow curved track in this way, they are mounted on pairs of underfloor trucks ('bogies'), each with a short wheelbase and able to rotate laterally about a central pivot fixed to the underside of the carriage underframe by a removable pin. Most bogies have two axles but some Pullman cars had three axles per bogie (12 wheels per car).

Colour light signals. Electrically operated colour light line-side signals diplay intense beams of light through coloured lenses to indicate to the driver of an approaching train whether the line ahead is clear. Railway lines are divided into sections, each controlled by a signal. Three-aspect colour light signals display a red light ('aspect') when the section of line ahead is not clear, either because it is occupied by a train or because a conflicting route has been set for another train. This is an instruction to the driver of an approaching train not to proceed beyond the signal. A yellow aspect indicates caution – proceed but be prepared to stop at the next signal ahead. A green aspect indicates that the line ahead is clear for at least two sections and that the train can proceed at any speed up to the maximum for that section of line. A four-aspect signal also exhibits two yellow aspects, which means 'two sections ahead clear but be prepared to stop at third signal.'

Coupling, buffers, gangways. The arrangements for joining vehicles together to form a train need to work both in tension and in compression. The traditional arrangement in Britain was for couplings – at their simplest a hook on one vehicle and a three-link chain on the other – to keep the vehicles together by transmitting tension forces whilst separate sprung buffers coped with compression forces. To eliminate the snatching effects of alternate tension and compression, a screw was inserted between the links of the coupling so that it could be tensioned to keep the buffers in slight compression at all times. The American Master Car Builders Association standardised on a single, central coupler consisting of a pivoted rigid bar with a semi-automatic clasp (the MCB coupler, also known as the Buckeye coupler after the Ohio foundry where they were forged) and handling both tension and compression forces. As American cars did not have buffers to prevent the snatching effect of any coupler slack, railroad 'engineers' (drivers) kept the locomotive throttle slightly open when applying the train brakes so as to keep all the couplers in tension – that is why steam trains in Western films continue to 'chuff' as they come to a stand. The so-called 'Pullman gangway', patented by the American company in 1887, consists of a vertical end-frame on each vehicle with a telescopic bellows arrangement that both provided a safe passageway from one car to another and a buffering function to improve ride quality. In that year the Pullman Car Company imported both the MCB 'Buckeye' coupler and the self-buffering inter-car gangway into Britain on three cars for the LBSCR. The design was adopted by some other British railway operators, including the Southern Railway, for its own fleets of locomotive-hauled stock. In 1925 the Southern had tried using MCB inter-car couplers on two fleets of new suburban stock but they proved prone to breakage in service and were replaced by an arrangement consisting of a three-link coupling chain joining sprung drawbars below the headstocks, tensioned against a short central telescopic buffer on the headstock of one car bearing on a pad on the headstock of the other. This close-coupling arrangement was not suitable for gangwayed stock so the Southern used conventional British screw couplings and side buffers for its express electric multiple units, including the Pullman cars.

Driver, motorman. Drivers drove steam engines, assisted by a fireman. Motormen drove electric multiple units and worked on their own. When steam locomotives were gradually replaced by diesel and electric locomotives and multiple units, drivers were retrained to operate the new traction but retained their 'driver' status. For many years the fireman – now termed a 'second-man' was retained as the member of the crew of a diesel or electric locomotive or a high speed train but eventually this position was eliminated with union agreement. With the move to universal single-manning the term 'motorman' was dropped – they are all drivers now.

First Class, Third Class, composite. From the outset, the fare structures and the passenger accommodation provided by Britain's main line railways reflected the class-based structure of the Victorian society they served. The promoters were gentlemen and were primarily interested in providing comfortable accommodation for their peers. As well as these First Class carriages, Second Class accommodation was provided for accompanying servants and for other less wealthy but respectable individuals. Third Class, where it was offered at all, consisted of the most basic vehicles, often open trucks, which the directors considered sufficient for the lower orders. In 1844 William Gladstone's Whig government passed the Railway Regulation Act which, among other things, required all companies to provide at least one train a day to all stations with covered Third Class accommodation, travelling at not less than 12 miles an hour with a fare of not more than 1d7 per mile. Despite the efforts of some companies to make these 'Parliamentary Trains' as unattractive as they legally could, they immediately captured 10% of the passenger market and Third Class travel expanded to over 90% of the rail passenger market by the end of the century, almost completely eclipsing Second Class. The Midland Railway led the way in abolishing Second Class and upgrading its Third Class accommodation to a similar standard. Because three-class travel continued on the Continent and therefore on boat trains between London and the Channel ferry ports, the obvious step of renaming Third Class as Second Class could not be taken until 1956. It has since been re-branded as Standard Class. Cars with a mix of First Class and Third Class accommodation were (and are) known as Composites.

**Multiple unit, motor, trailer.** Originally, trains were hauled by separate locomotives. Many still are, especially freight trains. The development of electric power for trains offered a new possibility – linking several powered passenger cars together and controlling them all from a driving cab in the leading vehicle. Typically, an electric multiple unit consists of a mix of powered ('motor') and unpowered ('trailer') cars – a 5-car Brighton Belle unit had two driving motor cars flanking three trailers. On the Brighton Belle the driver's controls were linked to the relays controlling the motors in the front and rear cars by a multi-core cable, with each wire controlling a different function – today's multiple units have much more complex electronic control software. Longer trains can be formed by coupling compatible units together, using a 'jumper' cable to provide through control to all of the motor cars in the train. Units linked in this way are described as operating 'in multiple'. Two 5 BEL units operated in multiple at busy times and a 5 BEL unit was sometimes coupled to a 6 PUL, 6 PAN or 4 COR unit to provide a mixed Pullman and non-Pullman service.

**Names and numbers.** From the outset, Pullman cars bore names, prominently displayed centrally on the lower bodyside and perpetuating a tradition of stagecoach days. These names were an eclectic collection, ranging from royalty and dignitaries through exotic place names to mythology. As we see in the text, the Brighton Belle named cars were less formal than those of other Pullmans of the era. Pullman cars also had numbers ('schedule numbers') to identify them in a register of company assets, particularly useful as names were often changed when cars transferred from one operation to another. On named cars, these numbers were only to be found on small plates on the ends of the vehicle. When Third Class Pullmans were introduced, they were not given the dignity of names but an abbreviated schedule number was displayed prominently on the bodyside as, for example, 'Car No. 1 Third Class', later 'Third Class Car No. 1' and finally just 'Car No. 1'.

**Parlour car, kitchen car, brake.** Internally, Pullman cars were generally arranged in saloon ('parlour') format, often with a separate compartment ('coupé') for larger groups or those who preferred more privacy. Some cars also included a small kitchen that catered for the occupants of that car and two or three adjacent cars. The term 'Parlour car' came to be used to describe any Pullman car that did not include a kitchen. Vehicles that included accommodation for the train guard have been known as 'brakes' almost up to the present day, even though continuous automatic fail-safe brakes on all cars were mandated by an 1889 Act of Parliament, replacing the system of individual mechanical brakes on some passenger cars, each operated by a guard in response to a whistle signal from the locomotive. Thus each of the two outer cars of a 5 BEL unit is described as a Driving (having a driving compartment) Motor (powered) Brake (guard's accommodation and a van area for luggage, mails and parcels) Parlour (no kitchen) Third (Third Class passenger accommodation).

**Third rail.** A system of railway electrification with an energised rail laid outside the two running rails. Trains collect electricity by means of 'shoes' mounted on shoebeams attached to bogies. The circuit is completed by returning electricity to the running rails, which are at earth potential on third rail systems. The third rail system was adopted by the Southern Railway as its method of electrification and was the system used to power the 'Brighton Belle'.

**Track circuit.** A track circuit is an electrical system to detect the presence of a train on a section ('block') of line and to lock the signal controlling the entrance to that line. One rail is insulated at each end of the section and low voltage electricity is fed to the rail – a.c. in the case of the Southern to avoid interference from d.c. traction return current. The supply energises a relay that enables the signal to display a 'proceed' aspect. When the section of line is occupied by a train its steel wheels and axles shunt the power to the other, earthed, rail thereby breaking the circuit and de-energising the relay, causing the signal to default to a red 'danger' aspect. Any failure of the circuit also causes the signal to revert to danger.

---

7   There were 240d (old pence) to the pound. A farm labourer's wage was about £35 a year in the mid 19th century.

# Appendix 2

## Train Identification

Passengers travelling by train between Victoria and Brighton in 2009 are reassured that they are in the correct service by scrolling displays on the outside and inside of each vehicle, backed up by frequent (sometimes too frequent!) announcements once seated. In Belle days, no such assistance was provided, but it is very unlikely that anyone mistook the distinctive 5 BEL units for a train to anywhere other than Victoria or Brighton.

Although primarily intended for railway staff, the front and rear of each EMU carried a numbered headcode to identify the service. The 2 NOL, 2 BIL, 2 HAL, 4 LAV, 5 BEL, 6 PUL, 6 PAN and 6 CIT units carried a set of stencils which could be placed over an illuminated opal white glass panel between the forward-facing windows of the cab front to provide the headcode. In contrast, the 4 COR, 4 RES and 4 BUF units built for the Mid-Sussex and Portsmouth Direct electrification schemes had a corridor connection at the end of each unit, and a white panel for headcode stencils was provided in place of the right-hand cab window, giving these units a 'one-eyed' look. The cab of each unit (the guard's compartment in the case of the 4 COR, 4 RES and 4 BUF units) carried a box with ten stencils, with one of each number 0, 1, 2, 3, 4, 5, 6, 7, 8, 9, to give a number series 0–98 (excluding 00, 11, 22, etc.).

The later EMUs of the 2 HAP, 2 EPB, 4 CEP, 4 BEP, 4 CIG, 4 BIG and 4 VEP series used a roller blind system. The Portsmouth COR/BUF express stock was fitted with roller blinds from 1962/63. In 1963/64 express stock was fitted with driver-guard 'loudaphone' equipment. The roller blind equipment could also display two red illuminated rectangles to denote the rear of the unit, whereas the stencil system displayed a blank white rectangle (not illuminated). When or shortly after the BEL units were refurbished in 1968/69, 3051-3053 were fitted with roller blinds.

The principal London–Brighton headcodes during the working life of the 5 BEL units are tabulated below. The Brighton Belle service was, of course, non-stop from Victoria to Brighton via the Quarry Line, and thus carried headcode 4. Note that workings from Victoria use an even number series (i.e., 4, 6, 12), and those from London Bridge an odd (i.e., 3, 5, 13)

### ROOF- AND SIDE-MOUNTED DESTINATION BOARDS

The EMU units built in 1932-38 for express working carried brackets on their roof, just above cantrail level, to carry origin, route and destination boards and/or train name [the cantrail is a narrow strip of metal or wood separating the bodyside of each

| 2 | Haywards Heath–Brighton |
|---|---|
| 3 | London Bridge–Brighton via Quarry Line (fast) |
| 4 | Victoria–Brighton via Quarry Line (fast) |
| 5 | London Bridge–Brighton via Quarry Line (semi-fast) |
| 6 | Victoria–Brighton via Quarry Line (semi-fast) |
| 7 | London Bridge–Brighton via Tulse Hill and Quarry line (calling at suburban stations) |
| 12 | Victoria–Brighton via Redhill (semi-fast) |
| 13 | London Bridge–Brighton via Redhill (semi-fast) |
| 14 | Victoria–Brighton via Redhill (stopping) |
| 15 | London Bridge–Brighton via Redhill (stopping) |
| 24 | Victoria–Brighton via Redhill (fast) |
| 41 | London Bridge–Brighton via Crystal Palace and Quarry Line |
| After diesel trains were introduced on the line via Oxted, the following headcodes were used | |
| 47 | London Bridge–Brighton via Uckfield |
| 60 | Victoria–Brighton via Uckfield |

Many of the headcodes were altered in the 1980s and since 2005 have fallen almost completely out of use

vehicle from the roof]. Brackets for smaller sign boards, showing destination only, below cantrail level were also fitted on the side of the driving coaches below cantrail level (between the driver's cab door and the guard's door). These provided additional or alternative identification of the service and were particularly useful in multi-portioned working. However, roof boards were rarely used after the 1950s, other on the Brighton Belle and the Waterloo–Portsmouth fast services because of the extensive inter-route working in the peak hours.

The 5 BEL units, when working the Southern Belle or Brighton Belle service, initially carried roof boards with 'Brighton Belle' in gold lettering shaded black on a cream background between 1933 and 1934, switching to the familiar cream lettering on an umber background, to reproduce the livery of the coaches, from 1934 until 1968. Bodyside sign boards were not carried on the units. After the repaint of the units into blue and grey, roof boards were no longer carried.

# Appendix 3

## Status of ex-'Brighton Belle' Vehicles at February 2011

UNIT 3051

| Car Name or Running Number | Schedule Number | Location | Status | Notes |
|---|---|---|---|---|
| 89 | 289 | Little Mill Inn, Rowarth | Static on site | In use as hotel Derbyshire Belle |
| 86 | 286 | VSOE, Stewarts Lane | Stored | VSOE Reserve Stock |
| 'Doris' | 282 | Horsted Keynes, Bluebell Railway | Static on site | Allocated to 5 BEL Project |
| 'Hazel' | 279 | Black Bull Inn, Moulton | Static on site | In use as restaurant |
| 88 | 288 | Ramparts C&W, Derby | Under restoration | Restoration to mainline use for 5 BEL Project |

UNIT 3052

| Car Name or Running Number | Schedule Number | Location | Status | Notes |
|---|---|---|---|---|
| 91 | 291 | Dufftown, Keith & Dufftown Railway | Static on site | Used as dining vehicle |
| 87 | 287 | Ramparts C&W, Derby | Under restoration | Restoration to mainline use for 5 BEL Project |
| 'Audrey' | 280 | VSOE, Stewarts Lane | Restored. Certified for mainline use | Operates throughout year on VSOE |
| 'Vera' | 284 | VSOE, Stewarts Lane | Restored. Certified for mainline use | Operates throughout year on VSOE |

Car 90 (unit 3052) scrapped 1995.

UNIT 3053

| Car Name or Running Number | Schedule Number | Location | Status | Notes |
|---|---|---|---|---|
| 93 | 293 | VSOE, Stewarts Lane | Stored | May be used as driving trailer for VSOE |
| 85 | 285 | Stored at Southall, London | Stored | Earmarked for 5 BEL Project |
| 'Mona' | 283 | VSOE, Stewarts Lane | Stored | VSOE Reserve Stock |
| 'Gwen' | 281 | VSOE, Stewarts Lane | Restored. Certified for mainline use | Operates throughout year on VSOE |
| 92 | 292 | VSOE, Stewarts Lane | Stored | May be used as driving trailer for VSOE |

# Appendix 4

## Pullman Car Diagrams

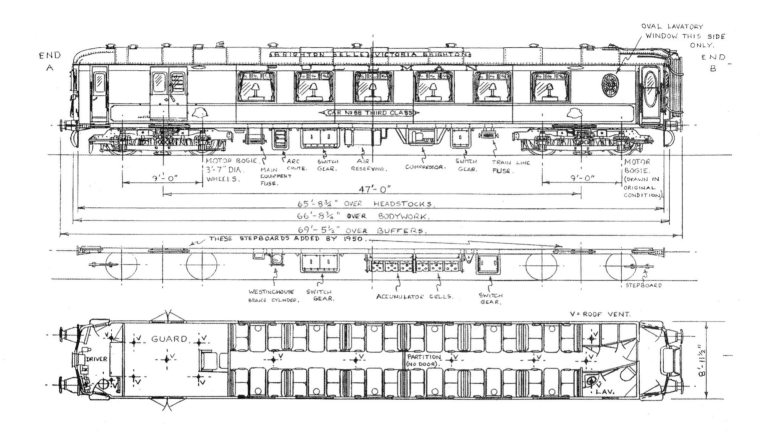

OVAL LAVATORY
WINDOW THIS SIDE
ONLY.

END
A

END
B

BRIGHTON BELLE VICTORIA BRIGHTON

CAR Nº 88 THIRD CLASS

MOTOR BOGIE
3'-7" DIA.
WHEELS.

MAIN
EQUIPMENT
FUSE.

ARC
CHUTE.

SWITCH
GEAR.

AIR
RESERVOIR.

COMPRESSOR.

SWITCH
GEAR.

TRAIN LINE
FUSE.

MOTOR
BOGIE.
(DRAWN IN
ORIGINAL
CONDITION)

9'-0"

47'-0"

9'-0"

65'-8¾" OVER HEADSTOCKS.

66'-8¾" OVER BODYWORK.

69'-5½" OVER BUFFERS.

THESE STEPBOARDS ADDED BY 1950.

WESTINGHOUSE
BRAKE CYLINDER.

SWITCH
GEAR.

ACCUMULATOR CELLS.

SWITCH
GEAR.

STEPBOARD

V = ROOF VENT.

V GUARD V

DRIVER

PARTITION
(NO DOOR)

LAV.

8'-11½"

5-BEL MOTOR BRAKE THIRD (LATER 2ND.)
PULLMAN CAR DIAGRAM 15B
© M. KING - 2010.

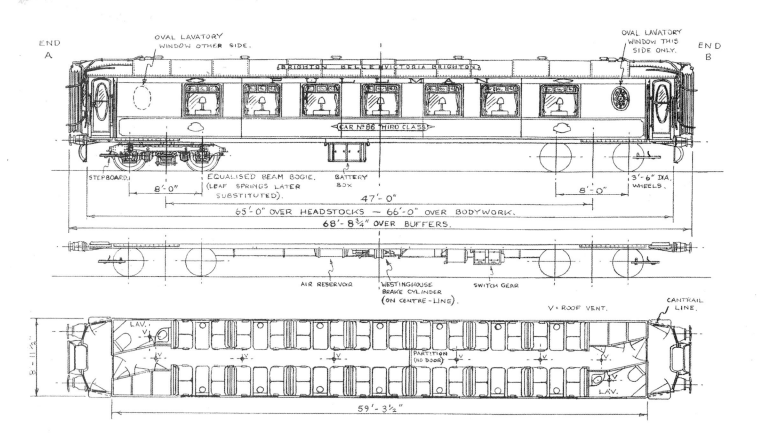

END
A

OVAL LAVATORY
WINDOW OTHER SIDE.

OVAL LAVATORY
WINDOW THIS
SIDE ONLY.

END
B

BRIGHTON BELLE ∘ VICTORIA BRIGHTON

PULLMAN

CAR N⁰ 86 THIRD CLASS

STEPBOARD.

8'-0"

EQUALISED BEAM BOGIE.
(LEAF SPRINGS LATER
SUBSTITUTED).

BATTERY
BOX

47'-0"

8'-0"

3'-6" DIA.
WHEELS.

65'-0" OVER HEADSTOCKS — 66'-0" OVER BODYWORK.

68'-8¾" OVER BUFFERS.

AIR RESERVOIR

WESTINGHOUSE
BRAKE CYLINDER
(ON CENTRE-LINE).

SWITCH GEAR

V = ROOF VENT.

CANT RAIL
LINE.

LAV.
V

V

PARTITION
(NO DOOR)

V

V

V

V

V

V

V

V

LAV.

8'-11½"

59'-3½"

# 5-BEL TRAILER THIRD (LATER 2ND.)
## PULLMAN CAR DIAGRAM 14P
### © M. KING · 2010.

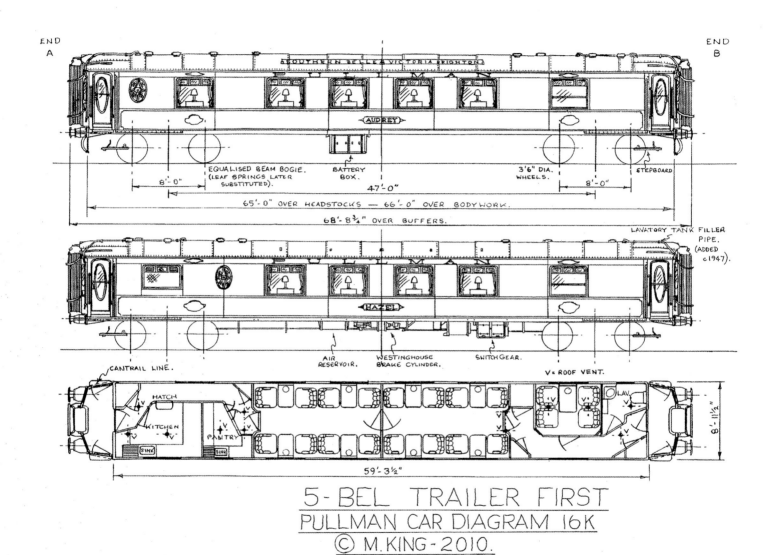

END
A

END
B

SOUTHERN BELLE · VICTORIA · BRIGHTON

PULLMAN

AUDREY

EQUALISED BEAM BOGIE.
(LEAF SPRINGS LATER
SUBSTITUTED).

BATTERY
BOX.

3'6" DIA.
WHEELS.

STEPBOARD

8'-0"

47'-0"

8'-0"

65'-0" OVER HEADSTOCKS — 66'-0" OVER BODYWORK.

68'-8¾" OVER BUFFERS.

LAVATORY TANK FILLER
PIPE.
(ADDED
c1947).

PULLMAN

HAZEL

CANTRAIL LINE.

AIR
RESERVOIR.

WESTINGHOUSE
BRAKE CYLINDER.

SWITCH GEAR.

V = ROOF VENT.

HATCH

KITCHEN

PANTRY

SINK

SINK

LAV.

8'-11½"

59'-3½"

5-BEL TRAILER FIRST
PULLMAN CAR DIAGRAM 16K
© M.KING-2010.

# Bibliography and Sources

Atkinson, J: '5 BEL units' – unpublished paper

Baker, M.H.C. 1989: 'London to Brighton'. Patrick Stephens Ltd

Baker, M.H.C. 1993: 'The Southern Electric Story'. Silver Link Publishing

Bell, R: unpublished monographs on the development of the Southern Electric network and fleet

Bonavia, M. 1971: 'The Organisation of British Railways'. Ian Allan Ltd

Bonavia, M. 1981: 'British Rail – The First 25 Years'. David & Charles Ltd

Bonavia, M. 1987: 'The History of the Southern Railway'. Unwin Hyman

Brown, David. 2009: 'Southern Electric Volume 1'. Capital Transport Publishing

Brown, David. 2010: 'Southern Electric Volume 2'. Capital Transport Publishing

Bye, Terry: 'Coupé News' (www.semgonline.com)

Bye, Terry 2010: 'Pullman Cars Preserved 1874-1966': 21st Edition (www.semgonline.com)

Carte, D., Kent, J., Hart, G. 1992: 'Pullman Craftsmen'. Queenspark Books

Cooper, B.K. 1981: 'Rail Centres: Brighton'. Ian Allan Ltd

Dawson, P. 1923: 'Electric Traction on Railways' in 'Railway Mechanical Engineering – a Practical Treatise by Engineering Experts'. Gresham Publishing Co.

Dendy Marshall, C. revised by Kidner, R. 1968: 'A History of the Southern Railway'. Ian Allan Ltd

Fryer, C. 1992: 'British Pullman Trains'. Silver Link

Faulkner, J.N. 1991: 'Rail Centres: Clapham Junction'. Ian Allan Ltd

Gray, A. 1977: 'The London to Brighton Line'. The Oakwood Press

Hamilton Ellis, C. 1960: 'The London Brighton and South Coast Railway'. Ian Allan Ltd

Haresnape, B. 1987: 'Pullman – Travelling in Style'. Ian Allan Ltd

Jenkinson, D. 1990: 'British Railway Carriages of the 20th Century – Volume 2'. Patrick Stephens Ltd

Kidner, R. 1998: 'Pullman Trains in Britain'. Oakwood Press

Lambert, Tim: 'A brief history of Brighton' online at http://www.localhistories.org/brighton.html

Lumley, John: unpublished data on Southern Electric fleets and operations.

Marsden, C.J. 1983: 'Southern Electric Multiple Units 1898-1948'. Ian Allan Ltd

Marsden, C.J. 1983: 'Southern Electric Multiple Units 1948-1983'. Ian Allan Ltd

Moody, G.T. 1979: 'Southern Electric 1909-1979': 5th Edition. Ian Allan Ltd

Morel, J. 1983: 'Pullman'. David & Charles Ltd

Morris, J. and Ford, A. 2007: 'Pullman Pride'. Noodle Books

'SCWS': 'The First Generation of Southern Electric Main Line Stock', article in Southern Electric Group's magazine 'Live Rail' Volume 7 no. 43, July 1978

Skinner, M.W.G. 1985: 'Croydon's Railways'. Kingfisher Railway Productions

'The Southern Way' magazine, edited by Kevin Robertson

Vent, A.P. (editor) 2009: 'Sussex Motorman – The Hubert Hobden Memoirs: Volume Two 1935-1961'. Buggleskelly Books

Welch, M. 2003: 'A Southern Electric Album'. Capital Transport Publishing

Welch, M. 2005: 'Slam Doors on the Southern'. Capital Transport Publishing

White, H.P. 1971: 'A Regional History of the Railways of Great Britain: Volume 2 – Southern England'. David & Charles Ltd

Winkworth, D.W. 1988: 'Southern Titled Trains'. David & Charles Ltd

*The photograph overleaf is by John Bradshaw*